PHILOSOPHY AND POLITICS

ARCHIVES INTERNATIONALES D'HISTOIRE DES IDEES

INTERNATIONAL ARCHIVES OF THE HISTORY OF IDEAS

113

ADRIAAN TH. PEPERZAK

PHILOSOPHY AND POLITICS

ADRIAAN TH. PEPERZAK

PHILOSOPHY AND POLITICS

A COMMENTARY ON THE PREFACE TO HEGEL'S PHILOSOPHY OF RIGHT

1987 **MARTINUS NIJHOFF PUBLISHERS**
a member of the KLUWER ACADEMIC PUBLISHERS GROUP
DORDRECHT / BOSTON / LANCASTER

Distributors

for the United States and Canada: Kluwer Academic Publishers, 101 Philip Drive, Assinippi Park, Norwell, MA 02061, USA
for the UK and Ireland: Kluwer Academic Publishers, MTP Press Limited, Falcon House, Queen Square, Lancaster LA1 1RN, UK
for all other countries: Kluwer Academic Publishers Group, Distribution Center, P.O. Box 322, 3300 AH Dordrecht, The Netherlands

Library of Congress Cataloging in Publication Data

Peperzak, Adriaan Theodoor, 1929-
Philosophy and politics.

(Archives internationales d'histoire des idées = International archives of the history of ideas ; 113)
Bibliography: p.
1. Law--Philosophy. 2. Hegel, Georg Wilhelm Friedrich, 1770-1831. I. Title. II. Series: Archives internationales d'histoire des idées ; 113.
K230.H432P47 1986 340'.1 86-8725
ISBN 90-247-3337-5
ISBN 90-247-3338-3 (pbk.)

ISBN 90-247-3337-5 (hardbound)
ISBN 90-247-3338-3 (paperback)
ISBN 90-247-2433-3 (series)

PRINTED IN THE NETHERLANDS

CONTENTS

Preface VII
List of sigla IX

Introduction 1
Notes 11

Historical Background 15
University and Fraternity (*Burschenschaft*) 16
Hegel's position and reaction 20
Hegel's targets 24
Notes 28

Schematic Rendition of the Preface 33
Notes 40

Commentary on the Preface 41
Paragraph 1–2 (p. III–IV) 42
Paragraph 3 (p. IV–V) 46
Paragraph 4 (p. VI–VII) 50
Paragraph 5 (p. VII) 52
Paragraph 6 (p. VII–VIII) 59
Paragraph 7 (p. VIII–X) 64
Paragraph 8 (p. X–XIII) 70
Paragraph 9 (p. XIII–XIV) 75
Paragraph 10 (p. XIV–XVI) 78
Paragraph 11 (p. XVI–XVIII) 82
Paragraph 12 (p. XVIII–XIX) 86
Paragraph 13 (p. XIX–XXI) 92
Paragraph 14 (p. XXI) 103
Paragraph 15 (p. XXI–XXII) 104
Paragraph 16 (p. XXII) 107
Paragraph 17 (p. XXII) 108
Paragraph 18 (p. XXII–XXIII) 112
Paragraph 19 (p. XXIII–XXIV) 115
Paragraph 20 (p. XXIV) 117

Notes 118
Bibliography 141

PREFACE

There is a didactical as well as a philosophical importance to providing a commentary on the *Preface* to Hegel's handbook on the philosophy of right. Considering the fact that the text brings us the thought of a great and difficult philosopher in a non-rigorous, "exoteric" way, it is well suited to the task of introducing students to the world of thinking. It is, however, too difficult to do this without being supplemented by some explanation. Analysis and hints for further study are necessitated here by both the interweaving of political and philosophical viewpoints and the philosophical presuppositions with which this *Preface* is full.

The philosophical importance of a commentary on Hegel's text can be found partially in the incessant quotation of the *Preface* in the literature on Hegel's philosophy to justify very different and contradictory interpretations. As long as the specialists do not agree about the meaning of the *Preface* to the *Philosophy of Right*, anyone trying to explain it cannot avoid the task of making his or her own contribution to the philosophical debate concerning the nature and content of Hegel's work.

This does not mean that any commentary can ever have the last word. For besides the historical, political, social and biographical backgrounds of the work there are other relations connecting it to logical, anthropological, theological and other scientific elements in Hegel's own works and in the work of others, relations which it would be impossible to clarify exhaustively. The introduction and the notes added to the commentary presented here offer an initial expansion of the text, but they themselves could be the starting point for new annotations – and so on into "infinity". For the author as well as the reader, then, this book remains a fragment.

I want to express my profound gratitude towards Mary Ellen Petrisko, Ph.D., for her translation of my Dutch manuscript and many quotations from Hegel's German texts. I would also like to thank the Dutch Organization for Scientific Research (ZWO) for its financial support of the translation and the Oxford University Press for its permission to reprint the text of Knox's translation of the *Preface* with some modifications. Ans Diepgrond and Rita Reijnen know that I am very grateful for their careful typing of this and other manuscripts.

LIST OF SIGLA

In this book the following sigla are used (see also p. 141):

An	G.W.F. Hegel, *Philosophie des Rechts. Die Vorlesung von 1819/20 in einer Nachschrift*, ed. by D. Henrich, Frankfurt 1983.
Briefe I–IV	J. Hoffmeister (ed.), *Briefe von und an Hegel*, 4 volumes, Hamburg 1961².
Dokumente	J. Hoffmeister (ed.), *Dokumente zu Hegels Entwicklung*, Stuttgart 1974².
Enc. or *Enc.*C	G.W.F. Hegel, *Enzyklopädie der philosophischen Wissenschaften im Grundrisse* (1830), ed. by F. Nicolin and O. Pöggeler, Hamburg 1959.
Enc. A	G.W.F. Hegel, *Enzyklopädie der philosophischen Wissenschaften im Grundrisse und andere Schriften aus der Heidelberger Zeit*, vol. 6 of the *Sämtliche Werke* (Jubiläumsausgabe ed. by H. Glockner), Stuttgart 1956³.
Enc. B	G.W.F. Hegel, *Encyclopädie der philosophischen Wissenschaften im Grundrisse*, Zum Gebrauch seiner Vorlesungen, Heidelberg 1827².
Enc. § 539 A	After a paragraph number A indicates the Remark (*Anmerkung*) on that paragraph.
Enc. § 6 Z	*Zusatz* (addition) to § 6.
Glockner	*Sämtliche Werke* I–XX, Stuttgart 1927–1930.
Grl.	G.W.F. Hegel, *Grundlinien der Philosophie des Rechts*, ed. by J. Hoffmeister, Hamburg 1955⁴.
G.W.	G.W.F. Hegel, *Gesammelte Werke*, herausgegeben im Auftrag der Deutschen Forschungsgemeinschaft, Hamburg 1968 ff.
Ilting	G.W.F. Hegel, *Vorlesungen über Rechtsphilosophie 1818–1831*, 4 volumes, ed. by K.H. Ilting, Stuttgart 1973–1974.
Lasson	G.W.F. Hegel, *Sämtliche Werke*, herausgegeben von Georg Lasson, Leipzig 1911 ff.
Wa	G.W.F. Hegel, *Vorlesungen über Naturrecht und Staatswissenschaft*, Heidelberg 1817/18 mit Nach-

trägen aus der Vorlesung 1818/19. Nachgeschrieben von P. Wannenmann, hrsg. von C. Becker e.a., Hamburg 1983.

Werke — *G.W.F. Hegels Werke*, Vollständige Ausgabe durch einen Verein von Freunden des Verewigten, 19 volumes, Berlin 1832–1887.

WH — G.W.F. Hegel, *Die Philosophie des Rechts.* Die Mitschriften Wannenmann (Heidelberg 1817/18) und Homeyer (Berlin 1818/19), ed. by K.N. Ilting, Stuttgart 1983.

INTRODUCTION

Hegel's book on the philosophy of right has two titles, divided over two pages. The left page reads: *An outline of Natural Law and Political Science.*[1] *For use with his lectures* (*Naturrecht und Staatswissenschaft im Grundrisse. Zum Gebrauch für seine Vorlesungen*); on the right page we find the title under which the book is always quoted: *Principles of the Philosophy of Right* (*Grundlinien der Philosophie des Rechts*).[2] According to both of these title pages the work was published in 1821 "by Nicolai's book store" in Berlin, but as is evidenced by a draft of a letter from Hegel (*Briefe* II, pp. 237–238), it had already been published at the beginning of October, 1820. The preface, written last, was dated June 25, 1820. Did the publishers postdate the book, which should have been published in 1819, in order to make it appear more recent than it was?[3]

The second title gives the best indication of the content of Hegel's book. "Right" (*Recht*)[4] is taken there in the very wide sense usually employed by Hegel. It involves not only positive law, studied in the various divisions of jurisprudence (civil law, constitutional law, criminal law, international law, trial law, etc.), but also the right which precedes and supercedes all positive law, for example the "right" of history, which lets nations and world realms rise and fall. Hegel's philosophy of right provides an analysis of the whole world of human rights and laws insofar as these constitute an objective realization of freedom. From one single principle he develops this system of law in all of its essential divisions.

The first title, *Natural Law and Political Science*, poses several problems. "Science" here is not opposed to "Philosophy", as is made clear by the second title. According to Hegel, a true, thorough and genuinely comprehending science can only be found in philosophy. It is only with respect to philosophy that we can speak of genuine knowledge.[5] The title can thus be translated either as "(Science or) Philosophy of Natural Law and the State" or – as appears in Hegel's course announcements – as "(Philosophical) Natural Law and Constitutional Law." *Natural Law and the Science of State* is a standard title used by Hegel for convenience's sake in the official announcement of his courses: During the winter semester of 1817–18 Hegel gave a course in Heidelberg on "*Natural Law and the Science of State*"; the course listing for the winter semester of 1818–19, given in Berlin, had the same title; for the winter of 1819–20 Hegel listed "Natural Law and the Science of State or *Philosophy of Right*"; for the winter of 1821–22 "*Natural Law* and the Science of State or Philosophy of Right following his handbook ≪Principles of the Philosophy of Right≫ (Berlin 1821)"; for the winter of 1822–23 "*Natural and Constitutional Law* or Philosophy of Right following his handbook"; for the winter of 1824–25 "*Natural and Constitutional Law*"; for the winter of 1830–31 "*Natural and Constitutional Law* or Philosophy of Right"; and for the last winter (1831–32) "*Natural and Constitutional Law* following his handbook."[6]

In his handbook, Hegel makes very clear that law is not divided into two orders or kinds, and that the state is identical to the totality of institutionalized law. The division which seems to be expressed by "and" is probably the result of the traditional philosophies of law from which Hegel got his title, but it is also possible that he wanted to thereby indicate the two primary parts of his philosophy of right, *viz.*, the first part, on abstract, preconstitutional law, and the first and main part of the third part, entitled The State (*Der Staat*).[7]

The term "natural law" (*Naturrecht*), which can be understood as an all-inclusive term implying constitutional law, is also a traditional expression, one which Hegel uses in spite of the fact that he claimed to find it "not altogether correct."[8] It is opposed to "positive law", the object of jurisprudence, and has been used since the time of the ancients to indicate that the law created by man is not the final word on right and justice and that it must find its source in something independent of human caprice. Positive law depends on a "natural law" (*jus naturale*) or "law of nature" (*jus naturae*), which is rooted in the "nature" (i.e., the essence) of man and society.

An explanation of the title "Natural Law and the Science of State" thus demands a rendition of Hegel's vision of the traditional relationship between "natural" and "positive law", i.e., a commentary on section 3 of his handbook, in which he defines what is *positive* in law – on the basis of the later sections 211–214. This is why in his later courses Hegel felt it necessary to give a commentary on this section at the beginning of his lectures on the philosophy of right, before he discussed sections 1 and 2.[9] As an elucidation of the title page, this section replaces the preface of the handbook in those courses. In fact, this is a much better place for section 3, for it is an irritating interruption in the train of thought provided in *Grl.* §§1–32. As Hegel indicates in the Remark on *Grl.* §3, this section is motivated by the intention of making very clear at the beginning of the book what can and cannot be expected of a *philosophical* book on right. To this end, it is necessary to define "philosophical right" (i.e., the right which is the object of the philosophy of right) as opposed to positive right or law, which is the object of positive jurisprudence. The latter contains all laws, rights and duties which together comprise the juridical system of an actually existing state. The former involves much less. For example, one cannot demand from a philosophy of right that it deduce all parts of an entire code of laws.

In his courses of 1817–18 and 1818–19, Hegel raises an objection to the expression "natural law" in that the principle of law is not found in nature understood as the natural world of the immediately given. In 1817 he even says: "The name 'natural law' (*Naturrecht*) should be abandoned and replaced by 'philosophical doctrine of right' (*philosophische Rechtslehre*) or [.....] 'doctrine of the objective spirit'"[10] Neither the external physical world nor the internal sphere of natural needs, passions and inclinations can be the basis of law. Spirit alone, more precisely freedom, is the foundation of the legal order. But "nature" can be understood differently, *viz.*, as synonymous with the "nature of the thing" (*Natur der Sache*), its *essence* or – in Hegelian terminology – its *concept*. If the word is understood in this way, freedom, too, falls under the "nature" of man and society, and right *is* something natural, since it comes forth from the nature of man. This "natural" law is then nothing other than the law and the right involved in the very essence of man, and its scientific explanation is identical to the doctrine of law insofar as this can be discovered and understood as a necessary moment in man's essence, i.e., to "the philosophical doctrine of right."[11]

On Hegel's view, traditional natural law did not understand that right is not the expression of (unfree) nature but of freedom. In his description of that tradition he is thinking primarily of its modern representatives, and in particular of Rousseau. Various of these individuals tried to base the social, juridical and political order on human needs, the satisfaction of which demands cooperation, or on a "social drive" (*Trieb der Geselligkeit*) which brings men together. Even when one relied – as did Rousseau – on a "drive for freedom", there was not sufficient realization of the fact that freedom is a polemical power and occurs as the opposite of nature.[12]

According to Hegel, besides having an incorrect foundation, traditional natural law is also characterized by a polemic against the actual legal system of the existing states. This is supposed to be an unnatural, artificial and corrupt form of law, as opposed to a natural condition ruled by natural law, which is considered to be an uncomplicated and innocent paradise. Nature is presented as a domain of peace in which man can find comfort for the corruption of cultural and political life. But these people do not understand that the world of the spirit must wrest itself loose of this innocence, because nature when left to its own devices is a primitive and animalistic world of passions, caprice and violence. It is thus not a question of dissolving the cultural system of right and politics in a "natural" society (or "state of nature"). As Hegel had already argued at the occasion of his *Habilitation* in 1801, Hobbes was correct when he wrote that "man must leave the state of nature behind him."[13]

In the *Encyclopedia of Philosophical Sciences*, the first edition (1817) of which preceded the above-cited course on philosophy of right, Hegel had summarized his criticism of natural law in a note (*Anmerkung*) at the end of the section dealing with "abstract right" as follows:

> The expression *natural law*, until now usually employed to mean the philosophical doctrine of right, contains the ambiguity of whether right is defined as something *implanted* by *immediate nature*, or something determined by the nature of the thing, i.e., the concept. The former meaning was the one usually intended in the past, so that a *state of nature* was imagined in which natural law was supposed to reign; the condition of society and of the state, however, demands a limitation of freedom and a sacrifice of

> natural rights. In actual fact, however, right and all of its determinations are grounded on the *free personality*, a *self-determination* which is the opposite of *natural determination*. [In the second and third editions (1827–1830) Hegel adds: "The right of nature is therefore the determinate being (*Dasein*) of the strength of power and its obtaining"]. A state of nature is therefore a state of violence and injustice, of which nothing more true can be said than *that it must be left behind*. Society, on the other hand, is the only state in which right has its actuality; what must be limited and sacrificed is the caprice and violence of the state of nature. (*Enc.* A. 415A).[14]

Many representatives of the natural law school maintain natural law as a critical test for positive law. Hegel integrates their intention in the introductory courses on the philosophy of right given in the years 1822–1823 and 1824–1825.[15]

Proceeding from the fact that right is primarily found in the form of the (positive) laws actually maintained in a state, and from the fact that physical reality ("nature") is also governed by laws, Hegel begins with the question: What is the similarity and what is the difference between natural laws and juridical laws? Both kinds of laws are found as given rules, which are "just there" (they are *Daseiendes*). It is in this existential mode that natural laws are studied by the physicist and the natural philosopher; in the same way, for the person interested in positive jurisprudence, juridical laws are nothing other than given, actually valid laws, which must be known.

The laws of a state, however, as opposed to natural laws, are created by men. They are valid due to an external human authority's imposing them. Natural laws, too, are imposed on us, but not by men. It is senseless to dispute their validity, for we cannot change them anyway, and we cannot replace them with others. With respect to the laws of a state, however, we experience an "inner voice", in function of which we evaluate those laws. We inevitably compare them with our own ideas as to what they should be. The measure of the correctness of positive laws does not lie in their simply being accepted by everybody or by a majority as universal law, but in ourselves. The fact that they *are* a certain way does not legitimize them. Only when we can realize that they *must* be as they in fact *are* can we consider them justified. But a conflict (*Widerstreit*) is possible here between "that which is" (*das, was ist*) and "what should be" (*was sein soll*)[16] or – to formulate the same opposition in other words – between "that which is" and "that which is rational (*vernünftig*)".[17]

According to Hegel, the question concerning rational law or law as it should be is not asked by positive jurisprudence but only by the philosophy of right. Only philosophy has access to the principles on the basis of which a critical examination, justification or rejection of existing positive law is possible. Only philosophy knows the criterion for the rationality of the laws which (must) govern the state.[18]

But two dangers threaten the philosophy of right. The first lies in every Tom, Dick and Harry's thinking that he is capable of criticizing the existing positive laws. Subjective opinions or feelings are poor instruments for determining what is rational and good. A proper insight into the elements and demands of freedom and justice demands a long and difficult endeavour. It is only true thinking which can lead here to a correct understanding.

The second danger consists in the prejudice which condemns the existing legal system from the outset, as if it were not the result of a long history of seeking and experimenting on which a great deal more sense and reason has been spent than is the case with the subjective prejudice that judges so negatively. In this respect, too, more effort is demanded to discover that somewhat hidden but true rationality which is invested in the current reality of law and politics.

Another danger which Hegel does not name but which he himself perhaps does not always escape lies in the ambiguity of the word "objective" which he uses in this connection.[19] Every positive law is an "objective" given, in so far as it is made known as a universal rule and must be obeyed by all citizens. Its objectivity is opposed to the subjective opinions and valuations of the individuals who must obey it. But the objectivity and universality of the *concept* and of the true and rational law is a different objectivity. It is expressed in an "ought" (a *Sollen*) that does not necessarily coincide with the "is" of factual laws. When Hegel polemizes against the defenders of the "ought", as we shall see, he cannot polemize against the criterion used by the philosophy of right but only against the "subjective" and individualistic interpretation of true rationality as it is grasped by the objective or super-individual concept. Hegel's philosophy of right is a critical theory, but it attempts to do justice to the juridical and political reality in an "objective" (non-subjectivistic) and "positive" (non-negative) way.

In *Grl.* § 3+A, too, Hegel makes it clear that one must differentiate between that which in itself is right (*"was an sich Recht ist"*), i.e., the rational (*"vernünftige"*) right, which *ought* to be, and the factual or positive right which only *is*. And not only because right can be *bad*,[20] but also and even more importantly because positive right is necessarily more extensive than can be philosophically deduced. The concept of reason only extends to a core of the existing law; the final concretization of principles of right which philosophy effects falls under other human faculties than those which produce the philosophy of right. It is very important that we remember this when we read Hegel's words on the relation of reason (*Vernunft*), actuality (*Wirklichkeit*), and present (*Gegenwart*) – especially in the Preface of the *Grundlinien*.

Right is "positive" in a pregnant sense in so far as it is neither to be deduced nor understood philosophically and yet is an essential part of a factually existing system of right. Although it is not immediately determined by reason, it can be good and just. But philosophy is not able to justify this kind of concrete right.

> It is a prejudice [to think] that the concept wants to determine everything: this is not true. There is an enormous sphere into which the concept does not enter; this field is given over to the subordinate powers.[21]

In light of the difference between "philosophical right" and mere "positive right" the intention of *Grl.* § 3 becomes clear. As Hegel says in the second part of his Remark, this section was added "to indicate the limits of philosophical right." One cannot expect a concrete and detailed code of law from the philosophy of right. It gives us something else, which is simultaneously much less than such a code and something more fundamental.

The fact that all right must be positive, i.e., that positivity is an essential moment of the idea of right, *can* be understood by philosophy. This is why the being-posited (*gesetzt*) of right in the form of positive laws (*Gesetze*) can be philosophically deduced in *Grl.* § 211–214 and anticipated in *Grl.* § 3.

The proof of the necessity of all right's being public with reference to its *form* and its being posited and executed by the proper state authorities presupposes so much that it cannot be given at the beginning of a philosophy of right. Nevertheless, Hegel can already show that he maintains a very concrete notion of right. The idea of right is no mere image, abstract thought or utopia, but an actual reality of a concrete human society.[22] The factuals laws of a historical state can be a distortion of true right, and thus a ruling "un-right" or injustice (cf. *Grl.* § § 211–212), but to avoid this danger one can only flee into the illusion of an other-worldly paradise.

Given the fact that "the law" is more than a totality of legal principles, it is also necessarily positive with reference to its *content.* There are three reasons for this, which result in three levels or dimensions in each concrete system of law.

The first element, which philosophy must maintain and recognize though it need not understand it, is the character peculiar to the nation in which the idea of right is realized. "The national character" is the product of natural and historical factors: to a certain extent these are contingent and cannot be philosophically deduced from the idea, but to a certain extent – *after* they have occurred – they can be understood.[23] As far as the *natural* elements determining national character are concerned, Hegel has tried (for example in the *Encyclopedia*) to thematize a number of "planetary", "terrestrial", climatological, geographic, and racial characteristics within the framework of a consideration of the "anthropological" characteristics of mankind.[24] The *historical* factors that have influenced the character of various nations must be studied by the science of history, and for this reason Hegel has attempted to justify a number of basic philosophical principles and relations in his *Philosophy of World History.*[25]

A philosophical explication of national systems of right includes the viewpoint taken by Montesquieu in his *Spirit of Laws* (1748). As is suggested by the sub-title of the work (*On the relation which the laws must have with the constitution of each government, and with morals, climate, religion, business, etc...*), Montesquieu understood that right and legislation are intimately connected to the other natural and cultural moment of a national history, together with which they comprise one organic totality (*Grl.* § 3 A). A proper interpretation of concrete right is only possible from the perspective offered by this totality, i.e., in so far as we realize that every legal system is the realization of philosophical principles *and* that it depends to a certain extent on geographical position, climate, race, popular culture and national history.

Besides being characterized by a particular "color", the right of a specific nation is also specified by the necessity of its application to all kinds of cases and objects. The principles of contract law, for example, must be differentiated in many ways in order to cover the various dealings of a particular society. This is not a philosophical task, because it is not a question of the internal unfolding or development of the fundamental concepts involved. It is rather a particular application of those concepts to matters, occurrences and relations found in the factual situation. Particularization through the application of universal concepts to classes or kinds of external givens is a task for the intellect (*Verstand*). The good lawyer is therefore someone who, guided by his intellect, is able to specify and apply the legal concepts of reason (*Vernunft*) correctly.

The particularization of right, two aspects of which have now been elucidated, does not yet make right into an actually existing, valid and effective system here and now. As a reality in time and place, the order of factuality is characterized by *singularity* (*Vereinzelung*). The factual is only that which is real here and now, and which in that sense is unique – occurring at only one time, in only one place. The final and definitive specification through which right first becomes real, determinate, existing and concrete in the full meaning of the term is the decision whereby it is applied and executed in one particular case. It will not do, for example, to sentence a murderer to "an imprisonment of three to 20 years"; the length of the punishment must be determined to the day and even to the hour and minute. The final concretization of right makes it an element in the order of the singular and contingent, in which the idea unfolds and incarnates itself. Philosophy cannot deduce the concrete content of the multiplicity of the singular or the dispersion of the contingent, but it can and must deduce and comprehend the occurrence of this factuality and its unclarity as something necessary. Considering the fact that the contingent factuality is the opposite of the pure concept, but at the same time its dark inner lining, as it were, by which the concept delimits itself, factuality is also characterized by irrationality, appearance and contradiction. Left to itself it would sink into a chaotic confusion and self-destructive struggle. Only in so far as it partakes of the rational principles of spirit, does factuality not perish but rather realize rationality.[26] In so far as the positivity of right involves an element of singularity and contingency, it also involves that inner contradiction. It is for this reason that Hegel defends as necessary the *in*consistencies of every legal system to lawyers who want to hide them behind a strained coherence.[27]

In complete agreement with his *Logic*, in which the necessity of the singular and contingent is deduced,[28] Hegel writes in *Grl.* § 214 A:

> It is reason itself that recognizes the peculiar, *though limited*, sphere and right of contingency, contradiction and appearance; it does not trouble itself to bring such contradictions into the equal and the just. What is important here is only the interest in *actualization*, an interest which is definite and decided, be it present in whichever fashion (within limits) it desires.

In his course of 1824–25 Hegel says that reason and philosophy cannot deal with all of concrete right, emphasizing the point much more explicitly than he does in section 3 of his book. In contrast to the impression that the *Preface* to the *Philosophy of Right* can create, we must thus forcefully assert that the factuality of the existing right *cannot* be understood or legitimized by philosophy in so far as it consists of casuistry and concrete decisions with respect to given situations. The intellect (*Verstand*) must do the best it can to solve the conflicts arising from various legal texts, but it can never complete this task. Every code of laws and every constitution are essentially and necessarily incomplete because the matter which they must govern does not allow completion. Empirical reality is in fact a "bad infinite", i.e., an endless multiplicity of contingencies to which in principle there can be no end. For this reason the "idea" of a perfect constitution or legislation is "a *bad* ideal." The concept (and thus philosophy) has nothing to do with the never-completed subsumption of cases under laws, because the concept is not finite: it is the infinite and completed knowledge of the concrete, particularized but true idea which is realized here and now.

With respect to "the final determinations" by which right first becomes actual, even the intellect (and thus positive jurisprudence) has no competence. Within the limits set by philosophy and jurisprudence some authority must make decisions. It does not matter so much which one it is. Indeed, the best legal system is worthless if it is not effectuated here and now. It is better for a nation to have a bad legal code than to wait for a perfect one. *Le meilleur tue le bien*,[29] say the French, but the Germans suffer from the illness of wanting everything to be perfect.[30]

NOTES

1. "Political Science" is the translation here of *Staatswissenschaft* (literally: science of (the) State).
2. *Grundlinien* (translated here, with Knox, as "Principles") not only implies the principles or foundations, but also the main lines of the *Philosophy of Right*.
3. In a letter to his friend Niethammer which he wrote on March 26, 1819, Hegel says: "For the Leipzig Book Fair I am to write another book (my natural law in §§)." See *Briefe von und an Hegel* II, p. 213. Cf. also Rosenkranz, *G.W.F. Hegels Leben*, pp. 330–331: "The edition ... for the bookstore was not done until 1821." Rosenkranz seems to suggest here that a first (unbound?) edition was available to students in 1820. – The external genesis of the *Philosophy of Right* is painstakingly reconstructed by H.C. Lucas and U. Rameil in a valuable article entitled "Furcht vor der Zensur. Zur Entstehungs- und Druckgeschichte von Hegels Grundlinien der Philosophie des Rechts", in: *Hegel-Studien* 15 (1980), pp. 63–93.) Much of the information given in this and the next chapter is taken from this study.
4. The German word *Recht* poses a difficult problem for the translator, because neither "law" nor "right" has the same extension and meaning. We try to indicate the exact meaning by paraphrases and explanations wherever the context does not suffice.
5. Cf. *Enc.* A. 5A; C. 16A.
6. Cf. *Berliner Schriften*, pp. 743–749. In the years 1802–1805, when Hegel was teaching in Jena, he announced a course in the philosophy of right five times, once under the title "jus naturae, civitatis et gentium" (natural law, civil law and international law) and four times as "jus naturae". Cf. H. Kimmerle, "Dokumente zu Hegels Jenaer Dozententätigkeit (1801–1807)", in: *Hegel-Studien* 4 (1967), pp. 53–56. In Heidelberg, Hegel announced for the winter semester (1817–1818) "Natural law and political science following texts dictated by the professor" (*nach Dictaten*); cf. F. Nicolin, "Hegel als Professor in Heidelberg", in: *Hegel-Studien* 2 (1963), p. 97.
7. At the beginning of his course on the philosophy of right in 1824–1825 (Ilting IV, p. 75), Hegel mentions this duality with reference to the double title of his book, but he quickly dismisses it: "In so far as natural law did not previously involve political science, it was treated separately". It is possible that with this title Hegel wanted to emphasize the fact that his "natural law" also included his entire political philosophy. Then we must read "and" as synonymous with "including". It is just possible that he wanted to point out by the non-identity of "natural law" (or law in general) and civil law that the state is not *as a matter of course* the same as the totality of all right, as is clear from *Grl.* §§330–360.
8. According to his first course in Berlin on the philosophy of right (1818–1819), shortly before writing the *Philosophy of Right*: Ilting I, pp. 239–240. "The name natural law is thus merely traditional, and not totally correct: since under nature 1) the essence [,] the concept [, and] 2) unconsciousness

nature [...] is understood.– True name: *philosophical doctrine of right* (*Philosophische Rechtslehre*)". In his course of 1824–1825 Hegel calls the name "natural law" "unsuitable". Cf. Ilting IV, p. 79.

9. See Ilting III, pp. 91–102 and IV, pp. 75–91.
10. Cf. Wa § 2A (p. 6) and Ilting I, pp. 239–240.
11. Cf. the lines quoted in Note 8. The following is a summary of texts indicated in Notes 9 and 10. See also Hegel's extensive article "Über die wissenschaftlichen Behandlungsarten des Naturrechts" (1802), in *Gesammelte Werke* IV, pp. 417–485.
12. Ilting IV, p. 79.
13. In his course Hegel quotes the expression "Exeundum esse e statu naturae", which he ascribes to Hobbes (Ilting I, p. 240). Cf. also Wa, p. 271. Ilting refers to Hobbes, *De Cive I*, n. 13, where we read: "Atque ita evenit, ut mutuo metu e tali Statu exeundum et quaerendos socios putemus [...]". The ninth thesis which Hegel had composed in 1803 ran:, "Status naturae non est injustus et eam ob causam ex illo exeundum" (cf. Rosenkranz, *G.W.F. Hegels Leben*, p. 159). In a course on the philosophy of history (*Die Vernunft in der Geschichte*, p. 117) the expression is attributed to Spinoza.
14. *Enc.* A. 415A. – Cf. also *Enc.* C. 502A.
15. Cf. Ilting III, pp. 91–93 and 96–102; IV, pp. 80–84.
16. Ilting III, p. 93.
17. Ilting IV, p. 81. Cf. also *Grl.* §212+A: "If ... so can the content of that which is law still be different from what is right". We translate *Vernunft* by "reason" *vernünftig* by "rational"; *Verstand* is rendered by "intellect".
18. Cf. also *Grl.* §212A.
19. Ilting IV, pp. 82–83.
20. Cf. Ilting IV, p. 85: "In this category [of *positive* law] we must also rank that which has come into a legal system, into a constitution by absolute caprice, authority, repression". On the other hand, however, we must also state "that violence and tyranny can be an element of positive right, are contingent to it and do not effect its nature" (*Grl.* §3A). The transition from rational right to positive right is the "place" where violence can come in, but neither the idea of *right* nor its *positivity* as such thereby becomes violent.
21. Ilting IV, p. 84. Cf. also *Grl.* §214A.
22. Cf. *Grl.* §1+A.
23. As is also evidenced by the beginning of the fourth Remark to *Grl.* §3 ("of the historical element first mentioned in the §"), what is stated in §3 under "*a*" must be read as follows: "through the particular *national character* of a people [*viz.*: 1] the level of its historical development and [2] the connection of all the relations which belong to *natural necessity*".
24. Cf. *Enc.* A. 392–394 with the extensive additions (*Zusätze*), which make clear that Hegel dealt with these matters in his courses over a long period of time.
25. Cf. *Die Vernunft in der Geschichte*, especially pp. 187–257, where Hegel also gives an extensive treatment of the natural and especially the geographic foundations of world history.

26. With my paraphrase I am attempting to show that Hegel's doctrine of the relationship between the idea (spirit, the concept) and the empirical order of the individual is strongly influenced by Plato's doctrine of ideas, chaos and participation.
27. Cf. *Grl.* § §214A, 216A, 3A toward the end.
28. *Logik* II, pp. 171–184; *Enc.* A. 93–94; C. 144–145 (+2); 213A.
29. "The better kills the good".
30. The commentary Hegel gives here in the beginning of his course on *Grl.* §3+A is a paraphrase of what he had written in *Grl.* §216A. Cf. Ilting IV, pp. 86–87 and 545–546.

HISTORICAL BACKGROUND

A complete understanding of the *Preface* to Hegel's *Philosophy of Right* presupposes not only a relatively good knowledge of his philosophy, including the philosophy of right which this preface introduces, but also an extensive familiarity with the political conditions and university conditions in which Hegel wrote and published his book. To satisfy this condition to some extent, a sketch is given below of the most important facts and occurrences that had an effect on the text of the *Philosophy of Right*.[1] To facilitate an overview of the events which are relevant for a good understanding of that text, the following chronological indications may be helpful.

July 1817	Publication of the first edition of the *Encyclopedia* (Heidelberg).
Winter 1817 – (14 March) 1818	Course on the Philosophy of Right in Heidelberg (six hours every week; see the lecture notes of Wannenman in Wa).
Summer 1818	Foundation of the Berlin *Burschenschaft* and of the General German *Burschenschaft* (student fraternities).
5 October 1818	Hegel settles in Berlin.
22 October 1818	First lecture in Berlin.
Winter 1818–1819	Course on *Rechtsphilosophie* (cf. the lecture notes of Homeyer in Ilting I).
18 January 1819	Order of the king's counsel: university professors manifesting a disposition dangerous to the State must be dismissed.

23 March 1819	Kotzebue is murdered by the student C.L. Sand.
August 1819	The "Karlsbad Decrees".
20 September 1819	Ratification of the Karlsbad Decrees by the Federal Congress (*Bundesversammlung*).
Winter 1819–1820	First Course on *Rechtsphilosophie* in Berlin (cf. the lecture notes edited by Henrich).
3 October 1819	Dismissal of De Wette from the university.
18 October 1819	Prussian ratification and sharpening of the Karlsbad rules on censorship.
30 October 1819	Hegel writes to his friend Creuzer: "I just wanted (....) to begin having my book printed (....)".
November 1819	Dismissal of Fries (Heidelberg), Oken (Jena) and Arndt (Bonn) from the university.
1820	Liquidation of the fraternities.
5 May 1820	Decapitation of Sand.
June 1820	The first part of the *Grundlinien* is sent to the printer.
October 1820	Hegel presents his book to Altenstein.
Winter 1821–1822	Course on *Rechtsphilosophie*.
Winter 1822–1823	Course on *Rechtsphilosophie* (Ilting III).
Winter 1824–1825	Course on *Rechtsphilosophie* (Ilting IV).
Winter 1831	Course on *Rechtsphilosophie* – interrupted by Hegel's death (Ilting IV).

University and fraternity

The reordering of political life in Europe which occurred after the Napoleonic period began with a mixture of modern and restorative measures. Most rulers in Germany had promised their people a written constitution; several had already provided one, or maintained the one introduced by Napoleon. The nationalism which had became so strong during the wars of liberation against Napoleon remained the strongest in the German lands, taking on the form among the intelligentsia there of a pan-Germanic movement striving for a German realm. Particularly in the universities did old and new currents make themselves known. Some professors made propaganda during their classes or at student celebrations for a more liberal political order. Popular sovereignty and representation, freedom and equality, constitutional monarchy, freedom of expression, and more of such ideas extensively paraphrased by the philosophers and essayists of the 18th century were popular among the students, but they were now mixed with a romantic enthusiasm for the German *Volksgeist* and the Germanic or "Teutonic" past, expressed among other things in the sporting of beards and old-German clothing. *Turnvater* Jahn, who expressed his love for the true Germany by establishing gymnastic (="turn") associations, was very successful. Many of the intelligentsia combined their nationalism with an anti-French sentiment and anti-Semitism. The call for a new Germany sometimes took on revolutionary overtones, but even those versions of liberalism which by our standards were very moderate caused great fear in most governments of the time. Little was realized of the more liberal promises made by various rulers, and the king of Prussia became very angry when reminded of his promise of a constitution.

One of the ways in which the striving for a united Germany was expressed was in the establishing of an extensive German student organization: the general German Fraternity (*die allgemeine Deutsche Burschenschaft*). A pan-Germanic society with political ideas and ideals, the fraternity arose in the place of the old *Landmannschaften*, in which students from various parts of Germany and beyond had joined together but which had degenerated into drinking and duelling clubs. The decision to establish the new fraternities was made during a student party held at the Wartburg on October 18, 1817 to commemorate two highpoints in the nation's history: Luther's posting of the 95 theses on October 31, 1517 (which is considered to be the beginning of the Reformation) and the battle of Leipzig, October 16–19, 1813, in which Napoleon was defeated by the allies. One of the speakers during this celebration of national enthusiasm was Jakob Friedrich Fries, who had been named professor of philosophy at Jena in 1816. Hegel quotes from his speech in his *Preface*.

Toward the end of the party, a group of students inspired by Luther's burning of a papal bull burned a number of reactionary writings by (among others) Kotzebue (a prolific and very famous writer and literary correspondent of the Czar, who had polemized against the French Revolution, Napoleon, the student fraternities and the gymnastic associations of Jahn), Von Kamptz (who was the director of the Prussian police), and Haller (a lawyer also criticized by Hegel for his reactionary ideas).[2] The establishment of a Berlin fraternity and of the general German fraternity took place in the summer of 1818.

The various German governments had become nervous. Fries was suspended from teaching due to his speech at the Wartburg, in which some had evidently heard revolutionary tones. Schleiermacher, who taught philosophy as well as theology in Berlin and who was a great friend of the liberal students, was forbidden to teach any more classes on politics. On January 18, 1819, a proclamation came from the king of Prussia commanding the dismissal of professors harboring feelings dangerous to the state.

The Prussian government, however, was not one monolithic reactionary block. It combined within itself both reactionary and enlightened tendencies. The king was indeed surrounded and influenced by conservative courtiers, among whom Wilhelm Ludwig Georg, Count of Sayn-Wittgenstein-Hohenstein and Minister of Police since 1814, played a major role. But Prime Minister Karl August Prince von Hardenberg was less conservative, and the minister of Culture, Education and Health, Karl Sigmund Franz Baron vom Stein zum Altenstein, was a liberal trying to make the University of Berlin a European center for science – for example by bringing Hegel there.[3]

Hegel had already received an offer from Von Altenstein in 1816, but he had not been able to accept it then due to his just having accepted a professorship in Heidelberg. He finally accepted a position in 1818 and gave his first lecture in Berlin on October 22, 1818, a year after the party at the Wartburg and in the midst of the political tensions in which the University of Berlin was steeped.

On March 24, 1819, the situation really became tense, when Carl Ludwig Sand, a theology student from Jena and a pupil of Fries, stabbed and killed Kotzebue out of his enthusiasm for the new Germany. After the slaying he tried to kill himself and was arrested.[4] At this point the police went on a rampage, under the command of Karl Christoph Albert Heinrich von Kamptz. Students were jailed; students and professors were taken in for questioning; house searches turned up documents; private correspondences were confiscated and examined. An attempt was made to prove that Kotzebue's murder was the result of a conspiracy, and that the university professors were corrupting the youth. The persecution of the "demagogues" was unleashed. It received a juridical basis with "the Karlsbad decrees", pronounced August 6–20, 1819 by a conference of ministers from nine German states and ratified in Frankfurt on September 20, 1819 by the federal congress (*Bundesversammlung*). The fraternities and gymnastic associations had to disband; government officers were appointed at all universities to watch over the political opinions of professors and students as well as over all appointments; all journals and books less than 20 quires long were subjected to a rigid censorship; a central committee was set up for all of Germany to investigate secret societies, and all professors who had ideas considered dangerous for the state were dismissed. The Prussian order of October 18, 1819 enforcing the congress' decrees sharpened the conditions on censorship: *all* books, without any restrictions, had to pass censorship.

Fries was fired in November of 1819, as was Oken, who also taught in Jena, and Arndt, who taught in Bonn. A riot broke out at the University of Berlin due to the measures taken against the theologian Wilhelm de Wette, a friend of Schleiermacher and an advocate of Fries' philosophy. The suspicions the police had about him could not be proved; on the contrary, he was strongly defended by the university senate and praised for his moderating influence on the students. But when the police found a copy of a letter that De Wette had written on March 31, 1819, one week after Kotzebue's murder, to Sand's mother, his fate was sealed. He wrote:

> You have received such a harsh blow as a mother that I feel obliged by your friendship to me to write you a word of comfort. If it were only the loss of your excellent son which you had to bear, I would remain silent, and leave the healing of your sorrow to your pious heart and time. But that the opinion of the masses will brand your son as a criminal, and with a semblance of right – this compels me, allowing myself a judgment on the matter, to plead his case to you and to protect his memory from dishonor, at least in his family.

Sand's deed "was the result of error and not wholly free of passion," but:

> the error is excused and to a certain extent abolished by the strength and purity of his conviction, and his passion is sanctified by the good source from which it flows. He was sure of his cause, he considered it right to do what he did, and thus he did right (...). It was the purest enthusiasm which filled him, one coming from the best source, but pushed by a youthful force it developed into a violence that went beyond lifes limits. Without a share of this kind of passion men can scarcely achieve great deeds; the light of enthusiasm will always flare up to a blaze (...). And whatever your son's fate might be, he has lived enough, since he has decided to die for the most noble desire of his heart... Do not say it is to be bemoaned that so many will not recognize the nobility of this death. At least it is an indication of a better view of life, by which some will be awakened.[5]

On October 3, 1819 De Wette was dismissed by the king without a trial. The university senate was very incensed by this, but could do nothing in spite of various letters to those in power. A number of professors, including Hegel, founded a support fund for De Wette, who had become penniless.[6]

In 1820 the fraternities were disbanded, and on May 5, 1820 Sand was beheaded.

Hegel's position and reaction

Hegel's work must speak for itself, but its interpretation can be assisted by the reader's becoming acquainted with Hegel's judgments and opinions as he expressed them in letters and in the deeds he performed. In his lectures and writings he sometimes exaggerates, and his polemics in particular can give a one-side impression to the reader. Some of the passages of the *Preface* to be examined here are examples of this. But their one-sidedness can be corrected by a fuller picture of Hegel as he reveals himself in letters and other statements.

Through a superficial reading of the preface to the *Philosophy of Right* and various passages of a body of the work, the impression may arise that Hegel is a stubborn defender of the existing order, and that he exhausts himself in apologies for the Prussian government's actions. Whether this impression can survive a careful analysis of his texts will only be answered after such an analysis. A good commentary can however be prepared by highlighting a number of non-conservative elements which are to be found in other texts – for the most part texts which Hegel himself did not publish.

An elucidation of the pronouncements contained in the *Philosophy of Right* by means of a discussion of the revolutionary ideas of Hegel's youth and his later praises of the French Revolution, Napoleon, fundamental human rights and constitutionalism must be a part of any interpretation which does not neglect the genetic aspect of Hegel's ideas on state and right. I shall however not deal with them extensively in this work.

As a counterweight to passages in which Hegel seems to approve of the government's actions against certain "demagogues" and students, one can point to his good relations in the years 1819–1820 with a number of leaders of the fraternities, men who were suspected by the police and finally were examined and jailed. Some of these were Asverus, Förster, Ulrich and Carové, the latter of whom was his assistant. To some of them Hegel wrote warm and friendly letters. He helped Asverus for years. On all of them he exerted a moderating influence, as a kind of mentor.[7]

It is very probable that Hegel did not want to ally himself to any one party but wanted to contribute in a careful way to enlightened, level-headed, non-revolutionary yet moderately liberal politics.[8] The politician who came closest to him was Altenstein,[9] who had brought him to Berlin and who hoped to acquire a place for him in the Academy (which never occurred, primarily due to Schleiermacher).[10] What Altenstein thought of Hegel can be seen from a letter which he wrote to Hardenberg on June 10, 1822, shortly after the difficulties sketched above and less than two years after the publication of Hegel's *Philosophy of Right*:

> I don't believe I may be too explicit concerning the excellent worth of Hegel as a human being, teacher and scholar. As a scholar his worth is known. He is certainly the most thoroughgoing and solid philosopher in Germany. Even more decisive however is his worth as a person and teacher. He has had an infinitely beneficial influence on the youth. With courage, seriousness, and a thorough knowledge of his field, he countered a deep-seated corruption with the solid exercise of philosophy and showed the youth the error of its ways. He is most honorable in his intentions and ideas, and even those who distrust philosophy recognize this, as well as his general good influence.[11]

In interpreting this letter we must not forget that Altenstein, writing his praise to introduce a request for an extra bonus for Hegel, also had an interest in proving Hegel's reliability. The letter also makes it clear that there were circles of government in which philosophy in general was not trusted. This fact will play a role in the interpretation of the first part of the *Preface*.

It would be an illusion to believe that Hegel exerted great political influence. Even in the day-to-day business of the university he had little to say, certainly at the beginning. Altenstein's power itself was limited, and he was unable to execute various plans due to the opposition of court circles or university figures. Hegel's influence in 1820–1821 would scarcely have been greater than in 1819, when he wrote to his friend Niethammer, who had asked him to support his nomination in Berlin:

> I have no one here to whom I could speak about it except to Marheineke in general... and he stands just as I do in the periphery, or rather outside it, without any relation to the effective and powerful sphere... I must also give you a brief idea of the complicated composition of the hiring machine we have here. – First of all there is the Department, with the Minister at the top; then there is the chancellor, with his advisory councils (which should nominate professors without the ministry's being involved); then the king, with not only his own very decided views on things and persons, but also his cabinet's...I am far-removed from all of these contexts.[12]

From this letter of March 26, 1819 we certainly do not get a picture of a powerful "State philosopher" to whom politicians would listen in awe; we do not even get the impression of a professor enjoying more attention than the ordinary respect of his colleagues.

The modesty of Hegel's position and the peculiar nature of his shyness can be seen in a letter written October 30, 1819 to his friend and colleague Creuzer, whom he had left in Heidelberg, and in one written June 6, 1821 to Niethammer. In the former, in which Hegel talks about the difficulties involving Fries, De Wette, Asverus *et al.* stirred up by recent political measures, such as censorship, he writes:

> You will surely understand that none of this helps to lift one's spirits. I am nearly 50 years old and have lived 30 of those years in these eternally restless times of fear and hope; I had hoped

> there would come an end to this fear and hope. [Now] I must observe their continuation – even, I think in dark moments, their aggravation.[13]

In the second letter, written after the publication of the *Philosophy of Right*, Hegel writes that he has weathered the "demagogical storm" without being endangered. At first he had been quite concerned and had feared being made the object of suspicion, but his worries had eased when he got to know a number of people on both sides of the issue. A reading of the infamous letter that De Wette had written to Sand's mother and the acquaintance of several demagogues had convinced him of their "wretchedness" (*Jämmerlichkeit*) and their well-deserved fate; the acquaintance with a number of government officials had made him realize that "in the beginning" they "indeed did not" act justly (but that was difficult "with such nebulous things"), but that they finally had shown justice in their actions.[14] There was now a new danger, but Hegel hoped to escape that as well: the king had forbidden teaching doctrines at Prussian universities "that lead to atheism" and "mislead the youth." ("You [Niethammer] know yourself how to sing such a tune", added Hegel sarcastically and without much respect for the king.) In the summer semester during which he wrote this letter Hegel was giving a course on the philosophy of religion, and he "did so in good conscience", but one never knows... The accusation that he taught pantheism or even atheism was at any rate later often raised against him.[15] Hegel ends with a general characterization:

> You know, on the one hand I am a fearful person, on the other hand a peace-loving one, and it is not exactly comforting to see a storm brewing every year, even when I can be assured that I will only be hit with a few drops of the drizzle. But you also know that being in the center of everything has the advantage of one's having more correct information concerning appearances and that one is thus more assured of his position and situation.[16]

According to Hegel, then, the situation was not so bad, although he experienced the persecution of the demagogues as a storm (for which the demagogues themselves for the most part were to blame). That Hegel did not feel particularly hindered by the censorship introduced (although in keeping with his character he was certainly careful) appears evident from the following announcement made to Creuzer on October 30, 1819:

> I wanted to begin having [the *Philosophy of Right*] printed when the congressional decisions [of September 20, 1819, ratifying the Karlsbad decrees] arrived. As we now know [after the publication of the Prussian order of October 18, (see p. 16)] where we stand with our freedom of censorship, I will now shortly go to print.[17]

Hegel's targets

Against whom does Hegel direct the polemic which governs the whole foreword of the *Philosophy of Right*, and especially its first half? He is clearest in declaring his disdain for the ideology maintained and presented to students by Fries, his former colleague in Jena and his predecessor in Heidelberg. In paragraph 8 of the *Preface* he quotes and criticizes a passage from Fries' speech at the Wartburg festivities.

J.H. Fries had become *Privatdozent* in Jena the same year as Hegel (1801); he had also become adjunct professor there in 1805, as did Hegel. In that year he received an offer in Heidelberg, where he remained until 1816. In 1816 he returned to Jena, but this time as a full professor. The place which he vacated in Heidelberg was filled by Hegel. Concerning Fries' activities in Heidelberg, Hegel said that he allowed the interest in philosophy there to practically die out.[18] This, however, is merely a weak echo of much harsher judgements which Hegel had made much earlier, long before the political developments concerning the fraternities. Thus on October 10, 1811, he wrote a long and devastating criticism to his friend Niethammer of the *System of Logic* which Fries had published that year:

> My feeling about it is in fact one of some distress – I don't know whether I'm becoming softer as a married man – that such a shallow person as he attains such honor in the world in the name of philosophy, and that he can assume such a tone – as if his writings had some significance? One can become irritated in such matters by the fact that there is no honest public comment in such affairs, for there are spheres and people concerning which it would be very useful. I have known Fries a long time, and

> seen that he has left Kantian philosophy behind, insofar as he has accepted it in its utmost superficiality and takes great pains to flatten and weaken it. The sections of his *Logic* and their elucidations have been published as separate works. The former, the § §, is dull, thoroughly shallow, empty, trivial: it is the worst, most disconnected classroom drivel imaginable, capable of being produced only by an idiot during the sluggish hours after dining.

Hegel continues in this tone concerning Fries' *Logic*, and goes on to ridicule his courses:

> I heard that his classes are seldom attended because while you are busy listening to one of his words, he has already tossed 12 new ones out. I can believe this, for his shallowness drives him on to pile 12 more words onto every one he speaks in order to dull the feeling in himself of his thoughts' wretchedness, and to bowl his audience over and thus prevent them from truly judging what he says.[19]

It is understandable that Hegel, irritated by the bad taste of the students and colleagues who thought Fries something special, took pleasure in exposing him in his *Preface* of 1820. The fact that he did not allow himself to be hindered in doing so by Fries' dismissal (in November of 1819) does not speak well for Hegel's sensitivity, but it does provide added relief to his opinion that Fries deserved to be dismissed due to his irresponsibly inciting the youth to imprudent political action.[20]

That Fries was admired by the students for his "progressive" politics and not for his scholarly or academic qualities was admitted by Fries himself in a later reflection written on his activities in Jena:

> The approval the students gave me was academically of no significance, for it was actually only political excitement that interested them and not at all my philosophical interests. My summons to them to do studies in political science instead of just talk in vague generalities were not very seriously considered.[21]

With reference to De Wette's dismissal Hegel had defended the position to Schleiermacher that the government might dismiss a professor if it continued to pay his salary.[22] In paragraph 10 of the *Preface* that we are interpreting here he seems to legitimate this position. Concerning De Wette, to whom Hegel proved himself a good colleague, his opinion was the same as that concerning Fries, whose follower De Wette was.[23] Concerning Sand, whose "most pure enthusiasm" so struck De Wette, Hegel judged much differently than his colleague. In a manuscript on the philosophy of religion he called "Sandian religiosity" a "purely selfish piety",[24] and as late as 1828, in a review of the posthumous writings and letters of his former colleague, Solger, he quotes with approval the following passage:

> It makes one shudder to take a peek into such a mind as this Sand's. He is certainly a well-raised, pleasant young fellow, for whom one must feel sympathy. But the *stupidity* of trying to save the Fatherland by murdering that old windbag! The cold, fresh arrogance, to sit in judgement of the so called wicked, as a little judge of the world: the empty *hypocrisy* of one's using religion, or rather its outer trappings, to justify the greatest atrocities! It is enough to make one despair in thinking of it! In the meantime, none of this is at all new to me. And I know exactly what the source is of it all. – They have been preaching to them for ten years that they are the wise and excellent creatures from whom the rebirth of church and state must come. – Stupidity, emptiness, arrogance: these are the spirits that move them, and they are true spirits of hell.

Concerning Kotzebue's death he writes:

> It provides us with a pathetic insight into the state of so many young minds. We find here a mixture of original goodness, shortsightedness (stupidity I would call it), arrogance, an unconscious religious hypocrisy towards themselves and others which makes one shudder. Can you believe that there are professors here who admire the empty coquettish bombast which the young man wrote to his family and friends? We remember all too well the nonsense of the Wartburg speakers and other such twaddle; still, as I said, we do not wish to blame anyone other than the spirit of the times. For a long while now everything has been going in this pernicious direction of wanton world-improving and empty arrogance, and many widely divergent doctrines have promoted it. – The unfortunate intellectual enlightenment with which so many are taken, the outrageous doctrine that the so-called agents of improvement must be and do everything and that everyone

> who believes wholly in this various world improving is one of these agents is the proper school of this exaggerated, mindless arrogance. One must fight against it with all one's might and at least clear one's own conscience.[25]

Sand and De Wette were theologians; Fries, too, had studied theology, and the great theologian Schleiermacher was a friend of De Wette, whom he defended in the difficult period after Kotzebue's murder. This type of theologians' theology irritated Hegel by its subjectivism, in which he saw the root of all evil. He analyses it under the heading of *Hypocrisy* (*Heuchelei*) in the long Note to *Grl.* § 140, in which Sand's deed is alluded to in phrases similar to those quoted from Solger.[26] "Piety reigns supreme" among the demagogues, but this piety is false. Their theology, widely accepted, was in Hegel's eyes an un-Christian emotional fanaticism. He believed himself to defend the true faith against these theologians' fanaticism, while their piety was ever ready to make accusations of atheism.[27] It had recently got to the point "that philosophy had to aid religious content against a certain kind of theology."[28] But the theology of feeling's political utterances were more widely attended to than their religious ones, and were much more dangerous due to their influence. Against this background we can understand why Hegel publicly accused this "barren [*kahl*, also "bald", Fries was balding!] and presumptuous sect", as he wrote in a letter to his friend Daub on May 9, 1821:

> With my Preface and the remarks I make there against them, I wanted, as you will have seen, to hit this barren and presumptuous sect – the calf, as we say in Swabia – right between the eyes. They were accustomed to having their say, and some of them were astonished that anyone could think nothing of them on a philosophical level and even have the nerve to speak publicly against them.

He added that this polemic had earned him "sour" and "silent faces" in Berlin, where that sect or party fancied itself a power and always had the final word. But he also said that people were not sure what to make of him or his criticism, since he could not be pigeonholed as belonging to the group of known reactionaries.[29] One could not accuse Hegel of going whichever way the wind blew. For even in his first official appearance as full professor, in his inaugural lecture on

October 28, 1816, in Heidelberg, where he had succeeded Fries, he had expressed the same criticism as in the *Preface* to his Philosophy of Right:

> ...the needs of the time... the interest of the great world affairs [the Napoleonic wars and the political re-ordering of Europe] have pushed aside a thoroughgoing and serious involvement with philosophy among us and frightened most people away from taking notice of it. This has caused *flatness and superficiality to take over and spread in philosophy*, since more solid individuals have turned to the world of praxis. One can say that philosophy has never had such a bad time since its beginnings in Germany, and that *emptiness and arrogance* have never thought and acted *with such superficiality* and such *pretentions* in this discipline as is now the case. To *counter this superficiality*, to work together [in?] German *seriousness*, honesty, and *solidity*, and to pull philosophy out of the isolation into which it had fled: to all of this we dare to say we have been commanded by the deepest spirit of the times.

In relation and in contrast to the grey theory which Hegel discusses at the end of the foreword to the *Philosophy of Right* as rising when the sun of a culture is already setting, it is very important that Hegel greets a contemplative *dawn* in ending the cited passage with the following words:

> Let us *greet together the dawn of a beautiful period*, one in which the spirit, hitherto torn outward, can turn back to itself and come to itself and can obtain space for its own realm, where minds go above and beyond the cares of the day and are receptive to the True, Eternal and Divine, receptive to the observation and grasp of the most high.[30]

NOTES

1. Cf. R. Koselleck, *Preussen zwischen Reform und Revolution*, Stuttgart 1975[2] and *idem*, "Staat und Gesellschaft in Preussen, 1815–1848", in: H.V. Wehler (ed.), *Moderne deutsche Sozialgeschichte*, Berlin 1966; M. Lenz, *Geschichte der Königlichen Friedrich–Wilhelms–Universität zu Berlin*, 4th vol., Halle 1910. Cf. further the very informative notes in *Briefe von und an Hegel*,

especially those of Volume II. See also P. Brückner, "... *bewahre uns Gott in Deutschland vor irgendeiner Revolution!" Die Ermordung des Staatrats v. Kotzebue durch den Studenten Sand*, Berlin 1975.

2. Cf. *Grl.* §258A and *Berliner Schriften*, p. 678 ff. (excerpts from Hegel from Haller's *Restauration der Staatswissenschaft*).
3. Cf. *Briefe* II, pp. 111–112, 170–171, 404–405, 409, 422.
4. See Brückner, *op.cit.*, pp. 42–48 and judgment of Sand by contemporaries on pp. 51–60. On p. 45 Brückner quotes the letter which Sand wrote to his family before his journey from Jena to Mannheim to kill Kotzebue: "The rise of the renewal of our German life began in the last twenty years, especially in the sacred period of 1815, with courage confided by God; our paternal home has been shaken to its foundations. Forward! let us renew our life and make it into something beautiful, a true temple of God, just as our hearts desire! Only a few resist, as a dam, the stream of the development of the higher humanity in the German people. Why do entire hordes allow themselves to be bent beneath the yoke of these wicked? [...] Many of the most profligate seducers play their game with us unhindered, to the complete ruination of our people. Kotzebue is the subtlest and most wicked of them, the true mouthpiece for everything bad in our time..." On Kotzebue see E. Benz, *Franz von Baader und Kotzebue. Das Russlandbild der Restaurationszeit*, Mainz 1957, and W. Promies, *Nachwort*, in: A. von Kotzebue, *Das merkwürdigste Jahr meines Lebens*, München 1965, pp. 295–315.
5. Cf. Brückner, *op.cit.*, pp. 98–99 and *Briefe* II, p. 445.
6. *Briefe* II, p. 447. For the whole history, cf. the extensive comments of M. Lenz, *op.cit.* II^1, pp. 34–176.
7. The givens concerning this are to be found in the excellent notes collected by Hoffmeister in *Briefe* II (Cf. pp. 216–217; 242–244; 330–332; 432–442; 444–448; 455–471; 498–502) and in the *Berliner Schriften*, pp. 581–584 and 598–607. V. D'Hondt has drawn a one-sidedly progressive image of Hegel on the basis of this material in his easily readable book *Hegel et son temps*, Paris 1968. The moderating effect of Hegel which is clearly and gratefully expressed in the accounts of Carové, Förster and Asverus is also attested to in a letter from Altenstein to Hegel from August 24, 1821 (*Briefe* II, p. 287) and one to Hardenberg from June 10, 1822 (*Briefe* II, p. 495). Cf. also Goethe's judgment of Hegel's pedagogical talent in his letter to Hegel of October 7, 1820 (*Briefe* II, p. 237).
8. Cf. H. Ottmann, "Hegel und die Politik. Zur Kritik der politischen Hegellegenden", in: *Zeitschrift für Politik* 26 (1979), especially pp. 252–253.
9. In a letter from December 11, 1817, Hegel says that Altenstein is "an excellent man" (*Briefe* II, p. 169). Cf. the judgment of Boisserée, who worte in a letter on September 13, 1824 that Altenstein was a "philosophical Minister" and an "Idealist as I have never seen among the businessmen of the higher class" (cf. *Briefe* II, p. 422).
10. Cf. on this point *Briefe* II, pp. 170, 179, 315–316, 449–450, 495).
11. *Briefe* II, p. 495. Hoffmeister's addition of "wenig" before "gründlichen Philosophierens" is superfluous. Cf. also Hegel's letter of June 9, 1821 to

Niethammer, in which he says that his position is very satisfactory and reassuring "in view of appreciation in higher places" (*Briefe* II, p. 271).

12. *Briefe* II, pp. 211–212.
13. *Briefe* II, p. 219.
14. An important passage, which well illustrates Hegel's independence: "I withstood the demagogical crisis without risk – but not without concern for those casting suspicions, slandering, etc., until I read De Wette's letter and got to know several individuals better, some of whom were demagogues, some of whom had to take measures against them, and thus recognized on the one hand the wretchedness and the well-deserved fate of the former, on the other the justice of the authorities, which in such nebulous matters of course is not evident at first but becomes so in the long run".
15. Cf. *Briefe* II, p. 268; the *Preface* of the second edition of the *Encyclopedia*; *Enc.* C. 573 A; *Phil. der Religion* (ed. Lasson) I, p. 254 ("... that the criticism is made of our position that it is *pantheism* ...").
16. *Briefe* II, pp. 271–272.
17. A precise analysis of this passage and of the facts on the basis of which it becomes clear can be found in the article by Lucas and Rameil mentioned in Note 1 to the Introduction.
18. *Briefe* II, p. 154.
19. *Briefe* I, pp. 388–389. Cf. also Hegel's opinion of Fries given in a footnote to the first edition (1812) of Hegel's *Logik* (I, p. XVIII, Lasson's edition I, p. 34): "A recently published, modern version of this science, the *System of Logic* by Fries, returns to its anthropological foundations. The superficiality in and for itself of the idea or opinion on which this is based, and of its execution, frees me from the trouble of taking any notice of this insignificant publication." Cf. also *Briefe* II, pp. 41–42, where Hegel says that the note cited was originally much harsher, but was softened during the correcting of the proofs.
20. Cf. *Briefe* II, pp. 218–219 (from the letter to Creuzer of October 30, 1819, cited above): "The political activities of the fraternity and De Wette's Friesianism have naturally not put the University into anyone's good graces. But it did not cultivate these seeds in itself; this has come for the most part from elsewhere and from where? –, primarily from Heidelberg; – seriously, the greater part of those arrested are those who were in Heidelberg before my time during Martin's and Fries' time there".
21. Cf. *Briefe* II, p. 444.
22. Cf. *Briefe* II, pp. 221 and 450.– In §144 of his Heidelberg course of 1817–1818 (Wa, pp. 215-216) Hegel states that a civil servant cannot be dismissed arbitrarily, but only by a formal trial and a judicial decision (*ein förmliches Urteil*). Not only judges, but all civil servants (*Beamten*) should have the right not to be dismissed. This constitutional right (*konstitutionelle Berechtigung*) is even "a key moment (*ein Hauptmoment*) in the organisation of the State" (216). In his course of 1819–1820 (An, pp. 257–258) Hegel seems to defend a viewpoint which is closer to the one adopted in relation to De Wette: the State can dismiss a civil servant, but in this case owes him compen-

sation. A judicial decision is not demanded unless the man in question has committed a crime. A court is not the proper instance for deciding whether or not someone has fulfilled his professional duties.

23. Cf. the letters quoted above from October 30, 1819 and June 9, 1821 (*Briefe* II, pp. 218–219 and 271–272).
24. *Philosophie der Religion* (ed. Lasson) I, p. 287.
25. *Berliner Schriften*, pp. 171–172. Cf. the quotations from Sand in Note 4.
26. In *Grl.* §140 under d (original edition p. 143).
27. *Briefe* II, p. 268.
28. *Die Vernunft in der Geschichte*, p. 41. For Hegel's relation to Schleiermacher see *inter alia Briefe* II, pp. 221 and 262; *Berliner Schriften*, pp. 81–82 and 684–688 and M. Lenz, *op.cit.* II[1], pp. 291–292.
29. *Briefe* II, p. 263.
30. *System und Geschichte der Philosophie* (publ. Hoffmeister), Leipzig 1940, pp. 4–5.

SCHEMATIC RENDITION OF THE PREFACE[1]

Paragraphs 1– 2 : Introduction
Paragraphs 3–11 : Polemic with the superficial philosophy of state and right
Paragraphs 12–19 : The proper relation of philosophy of right to to reality
Paragraph 20 : Conclusion

Introduction (par. 1–2)

Par. 1 : This is a guide and a textbook
Par. 2 : But it is not an ordinary compendium, because:
- the remarks are too extensive;
- an ordinary compendium contains only that which is cut and dried and well-known.

PART I (par. 3–11): Polemic with superficial philosophy of right, which occasions so much falsehood and trouble

I. Proper and improper methods (par. 3–5)

Par. 3 : (This is no ordinary compendium) due to the *speculative method* used here (a)
(b) The ordinary method now is:
- directed against the old logic (of the intellect (*Verstand*));

– a caprice of emotion, intuition and imagination, combined with ordinary argumentation and reasoning.

(a) The nature of speculative knowledge is *different*: in science, the *content* is essentially bound to the *form*.

Par. 4 : (Form and content are identical, cf. par. 18)

(b) Their theory is: Form is unimportant; matter (content; truths) is what counts. Their practice is merely a rehashing:

– This is valuable for education (*Bildung*).
– It is superfluous: the ancients said it before, and better.

(a) Hegel's critique of (b):

– How pretentious! They are saying nothing new.
– The conflicts in their self-contradictory truths can only be solved by (the form of) science.

Par. 5 : – The truth concerning right and rationality is
– old
– public and well-known.

Given by external and internal authorities, this truth merely needs to be understood and justified by thought.

II. The relation of the subject to rational reality (par. 6–9)

Par. 6 : 1. (a) The unprejudiced mind trusts in the publicly known truth of morality.

(b) A supposed difficulty: How can one find the universally valid in so many different opinions?
Critique: This difficulty betrays the vanity and individuality of their thinking and being.

2. (a) A further difficulty: Thinking is freedom/ the search for the basis of morality.

(b) This right becomes an injustice when one identifies thinking and freedom with the deviation from the generally-accepted and the discovery of something particular.

Par. 7 : 3. (b) It is especially with reference to the state that this incorrect notion on philosophy's part is widely held today: some philosophers act as if there were as yet no state and they had to invent it.

α) *Refutation of the idea that the state is not an actual rationality*:

– With reference to *nature*, it is admitted that philosophy must understand actual reason as its immanent law and essence.

– With reference to the *moral world* (i.e. reason as as it realizes itself in self-consciousness), on the other hand, it is believed:

aa) that this is not a rational reality, but rather one subject to chance and caprice: moral atheism;

bb) the true is found outside the moral world, and is merely a problem;

cc) for these reasons everyone may and must figure out this truth (not "seek" it, for everyone already possesses the philosopher's stone).

– As far as their intellect and will are concerned many/all people are satisfied with the actual state. At least those people who are aware of this satisfaction laugh at the claims cited above and see them as a game.

β) *Refutation of an incorrect conception of philosophy* (whence the above mentioned misconception springs):

– This "game" (however is not without dangers, for it) brings philosophy into discredit.

– The worst contempt for philosophy consists in (everyone's conviction that he can do it (→ par. 10)

Par. 8 : – Indeed:

(b) Contemporary political philosophy is such that anyone could think it up. In fact it says itself that truth cannot be known, and at the same time that the true is that which springs from everyone's heart and spirit (fodder for youth and sleepers). The person who introduced this nonsense is Fries (quotation from his Wartburg speech).

(a) Science is the development of the concept. It is in science that the state shows its rational architectonic.

(b) Superficiality dissolves this in the morass of heart and spirit and the subjective contingency of opinion and caprice; it bases on feeling that which is the result of a long historical process of the intellect and reason.
(Thus it saves itself all the trouble of scientific thinking. "Only have contempt.."

γ) *Return to (a): In the name of religious truths, some despise the existing moral reality*:

(b) Superficiality dresses itself in robes of piety and despises the objective laws in the name of the Bible.

(a) True piety is a simple and emotional intuition of the truth, but it relinquishes its subjectivity as soon as it steps into the light of the developed idea. It reveres the objective truth of the law.

Par. 9 : 4. (b) Subjectivistic philosophy is a special form of guilty conscience. "Spirit", "life", "folk", etc. must hide its spiritlessness, selfishness and arrogance. The true shibboleth, however, is: hatred of the law, i.e., subjective conviction over against the comprehended rationality of right and rationality in the form of law and duty.

III. Reactions of the state to this philosophy (par. 10–11a)

Par. 10 : The distortion of philosophy to a capricious opinion has cast suspicion on all political philosophy (cf. par. 7, β) and understandably provoked the government.

1. *First reason for the government's reaction*:

– Philosophy here [in Germany] is not a private matter, but a public one, (especially or solely in service of the state).

- Governments have shown confidence in philosophy (in which cases they have often been poorly repaid) or have been indifferent to it (and then they have had to suffer from the disappearance of thorough knowledge).
- Superficiality (which does not get to the real substance) does not seem to harbor any danger for external law and order.

  But: The state needs thoroughgoing education, insight and science. Superficiality leads to sophism and subjectivism, which destroy the foundations of morality, the just conscience, love and right in the private sphere, and public order.
  - Against governmental measures, superficiality claim the support of acquired confidence authority of one's office.

Par. 11 : 2. *Second reason for the government being concerned with philosophy*:

The proper exercise of philosophy has developed a need for governmental protection and help. For its public existence is threatened by anti-philosophical exclamations for the positive sciences, edifying and other literature. It seems tradition is no longer sufficient to guarantee the tolerance philosophy or its public existence.

IV. Concluding characterization and judgment of bad political philosophy (par. 11b)

The "philosophical" attacks on philosophy are based equally on the superficiality characterized here and the philosophical element against which they fulminate. By declaring knowledge of the truth to be impossible, they are despotic – just as the Roman emperor who levels everything. The result of their despotic subjectivism is that the moral laws are just as truc as thc most criminal convictions.

PART II (par. 12–19): On the relation of political philosophy to the reality of the state

I. The relation of philosophy to reality in general (par. 12–13)

Par. 12 : – Transition from Part I (the opposition of bad and true philosophy) to Part II:
the break between philosophy and reality is:
aa) a happy circumstance;
bb) necessary due to the nature of the matter.
The misunderstandings (discussed in Part I) are concerned with precisely the relation of philosophy to reality (cf. par. 7)

– *Thesis*: The proper conception is:
Philosophy is + the fathoming of the rational;
+ the grasping of present reality;
+ not a positing of a *Jenseits*.

– *Illustration*: Even Plato's *Republic* was a grasping of the (then) present reality (i.e. of the existing struggle between the ancient, perfect principle of the classic *polis* and the new, as yet abstract principle of individual subjectivity).

Par. 13 : – The basis of the proper conception is the reciprocal implication of the rational and the actual.

+ This is the conviction of every unprejudiced consciousness.
+ (b) The subjectivistic consciousness is of the opinion that the present is idle and empty and that the idea is a subjective representation, but this consciousness is itself idle and empty.
+ (a) Philosophy understands that eternal substance is actually present in the appearance of the temporal. For, the idea (the rational, the heart, the pulse, the essence) actualizes itself in the external existence of the phenomena (multi-colored exterior, external forms, appearance)).
The object of philosophy is not the appearance of essence, but the idea.
+ (b) This is why there is a radical difference between philosophy and idle "know-it-allness".

II. The relation of political philosophy to the existing state (par. 14–19)

Par. 14 : 1. *Consequence of I*: Political philosophy is to understand state as a rational universe, not construct a state as it *ought* to be.

Par. 15 : – *Hic Rhodus...*
Philosophy = understanding what is, for what is, is reason.
– (*Philosophy itself is historical*):
(a) Philosophy is its time caught in thought.
(b) A world such as it *ought* to be exists only in opinion.

Par. 16 : – *Hier ist die Rose, hier tanze* (Here is the rose, dance here).

Par. 17 : 2. The opposition between (reason as) self-aware spirit and (reason as) present reality has two solutions.
(b) Division : comes from an abstract reflection and leads to dissatisfaction.
(a) Unity : reason knows and recognizes the rose in the cross of the present reality: reconciliation of subjective freedom and substance.

Par. 18 : 3. (*Translation of this unity and reconciliation in terms of par. 4*)
The idea is the unity of form (reason as comprehensible knowledge) and content (reason as the substantial essence of natural and moral realities).
4. (*The relative correctness of the opponent*)
– The principle of modernity and Protestantism is that a free human can only agree with that which is justified by thought.
– The concept is the same as Luther's belief and witness of the spirit.
– A half philosophy (cf. par. 7: the atheism of the moral world) leads away from God and State; true philosophy leads to them and attains true peace.

Par. 19 : 5. Philosophy always comes too late to teach the world how it *ought* to be (cf. par. 14).
Philosophy is the idea of a complete reality. This truth is proved by the concept as well as by history. The ideal ap-

pears next to the real when a form of life has grown old. It paints in grey tones the substance of a complete form of life. Its knowledge is not rejuvenation, but a reflection. "The owl of Minerva...."

Conclusion (par. 20)

Par. 20 : As a preface, this preface was an external and subjective discussion. A philosophical treatment and a philosophical critique should be objective.

NOTES

1. As I hope to prove in another study on Hegel's work, the structure according to which he composed his texts is an integral part of his argumentation. The polemic character of the *Preface* is here shown by the letters (a) and (b) within parentheses: Hegel's own position is marked by (a); positions attacked by him are indicated by (b).

COMMENTARY ON THE PREFACE

The *Preface*[1] to the *Principles of the Philosophy of Right*, which Hegel finished on June 25, 1829 and undoubtedly wrote after having edited the rest,[2] contains not a "scientific treatment of the matter itself", but an "external and subjective" presentation (par. 20) in which Hegel wishes to realize two objectives. First of all, as is the case in his other Forewords or Introductions, he wants to indicate in a non-technical and preliminary fashion what the reader should expect from a philosophical treatise, how it should be read, and on which level and with which method it functions.[3] A positive explication of the peculiar nature of philosophical thinking concerning right is given by Hegel particularly in the second part of this *Preface* (par. 12–19). Due to the fact that most "philosophers" of his time did not practice the true way of thinking, however, Hegel precedes this with a polemic. In paragraphs 3–11 he compares his true, speculative thought to another major current, one which was well received and therefore all the more dangerous: a philosophy of feeling, with great pretentions, one of the philosophies of immediate knowing,[4] of which J.H. Fries was an infamous example. The examination of this "superficial" philosophy is concerned not only with its theoretical aspects but, since it is a philosophy of right and state, with its practical consequences as well. Fries engaged himself politically by acting as the ideologist of the fraternities. Others, such as the theologian De Wette, also translated their theory into a political position. Both Fries and De Wette were dismissed, causing great upheaval at the university.

For Hegel, the political developments and *petite histoire* of 1819 were a reason for discussing the more fundamental problem of the relation of philosophy of right on the one hand and state and the political and juridical reality on the other. His positive remarks on this relation are made in the second part of the work (par. 12–19), while paragraphs 10–11 in particular discuss the conflict between those holding political power and bad philosophy. With this discussion Hegel realizes his second objective: he takes a stand regarding an issue which is both political and philosophical. The two intentions out of which the *Preface* grew and the two parts (par. 3–11 and par. 12–19 respectively) of which it consists are united by the fact that philosophy and politics cannot operate independently of one another, as Plato had already understood, and that sophists are a great danger to the state.

The uniting of a theoretical and a political intention, however, results in Hegel's directing himself to two audiences at the same time in this *Preface*: 1) to colleagues and students, to whom he explains what philosophy is (specifically: philosophizing on right and politics); 2) to the government and politically engaged citizens (e.g., the fraternity members), to whom he wishes to explain which policy is the proper one concerning philosophers and philosophy. An additional factor is that he is working here in a non-scientific way, i.e., hypothetically and without proofs ("externally and subjectively"), so that what he says has more a rhetorical than philosophical character. As we will see, this mixing of aspects results in a certain ambiguity.[5] To discover the well-hidden meaning of a number of statements, one must start with the texts in which Hegel *does* proceed in a scientific fashion and speaks to philosophers or students of philosophy. Just as he wrote the *Preface* after the actual work, so, too, must the reader understand it after studying this work (and other works on which it is based). A commentary on the *Preface* could in this way be saved for the end. If it is given at the beginning, it will necessarily contain anticipations and unproved claims. A partial remedy for the unproved character of certain statements, which thus becomes inevitable, consists in references to sections of the actual philosophy of right, which will be treated later.

Paragraph 1–2 (p. III–IV)

> The immediate inducement to publish this compendium is the need for putting into the hands of my audience a guide for the lectures on the Philosophy of Right which I deliver in accordance with my office. This textbook is a more extensive and especially a more systematic exposition of the

same fundamental concepts which in relation to this part of philosophy are already contained in a book of mine designed previously for my lectures – the *Encylopaedia of Philosophical Sciences* (Heidelberg, 1817).

But this compendium was to appear in print and therefore it now comes before the general public; and this was my inducement to amplify here a good many of the Remarks which were primarily meant in a brief compass to indicate ideas akin to my argument or at variance with it, further inference from it, and the like, i.e. material which would receive its requisite elucidation in my lectures. The object of amplifying them here was to clarify occasionally the more abstract parts of the text and to take a more comprehensive glance at related ideas widely disseminated at the present time. Hence the result has been a number of Remarks rather more extensive than is usually consistent with the style and aim of a compendium. Apart from that, however, a compendium proper has as its subject-matter what is taken to be the closed circle of science; and what is appropriate in it, except perhaps for a small addition here and there, is principally the assembly and arrangement of the essential factors in a content which has long been familiar and accepted, just as the form in which it is arranged has its rules and artifices which have long been settled. *Philosophical* compendia are perhaps not now expected to conform to such a pattern, for it is supposed that what philosophy puts together is a work as ephemeral as Penelope's web, one which must be begun afresh every morning.[6]

The *Preface* begins with a simple statement of Hegel's reason for writing his outline or compendium (*Grundriss*). The *Encylopedia of Philosophical Sciences in Outline*, which Hegel had published in June 1817 as a handbook for his courses in Heidelberg, contains a section on the philosophy of right (A. 400–452) under the heading *Objective Spirit*. Hegel used this text as a handbook in his courses on "Natural Law and State Law" (*Natur- und Staatsrecht*), given in the winter semester of 1817–1818 in Heidelberg and in the winter semester of 1818–1819 in Berlin. During the latter he wrote a large number of notes in his own interleaved copy of the third part of the *Encyclopedia*,[7] as he also did on its sections on *Subjective Spirit*, which he used as a compendium for the course he often gave on that subject. It is possible that Hegel wanted to write a more extensive treatise on both subjective and objective spirit,[8] but it was only on the latter that he in fact wrote a separate book. In comparison to the Heidelberg version, subjective spirit received a much more extensive treatment in the second and third editions of the *Encyclopedia* (of 1827 and 1830, respectively).[9]

The reason why Hegel published a separate book on the philosophy of right is formulated in paragraph 1: it provides a more extensive and more systematic explanation of the same principles developed in *Enc.* A. 400–452. Although a comparison of the contents of the *Philosophy of Right* and the Heidelberg edition of the *Encyclopedia* reveals considerable differences,[10] Hegel states that both texts treat the same principles. The quintessence of their legal principles is indeed the same. But Hegel wants to develop this concept "more extensively" and "more systematically." The conceptual and systematic structure must be brought out in more detail. What this means exactly can only be ascertained by analyzing and comparing the systematic or "logical" aspects of both texts. For the time being we must be satisfied with the words "more extensive"[11] and a vague notion of "more systematic". A seemingly unimportant detail of the first paragraph is Hegel's assertion that he is giving courses on the philosophy of law "in accordance with his office".[12] With paragraphs 10–11, however, it will become clear that philosophy practised as a (state) office has a political dimension *ipso facto*, and that it cannot avoid the political necessities of the state. The beginning of the *Preface* thus introduces the main idea of the work in an inconspicuous way – that idea being the theoretical and practical relation of political reality and the philosophy of right.

In the second paragraph, which sets itself off from the first by the word "but", Hegel remarks that his book is not a compendium in the ordinary sense of the term. There are two reasons for this.

The first reason is given in the first three sentences. The nature of a compendium is such that it only organizes and summarizes the basic lines and principles of an already known and accepted subject matter. In so doing, it can also contain some remarks on less essential topics, such as the relation between what is said and related or divergent ideas, consequences, etc.. Extensive commentaries on its subdivisions, however, do not fit in with the purpose and style of a compendium: they belong in the courses for which the compendium serves as a handbook. The *Philosophy of Right*, however, contains extensive *Remarks*, e.g., on other contemporary theories. Because the text which Hegel wrote "for use with his lectures" (according to the first title page) was published (there was no other means for quick reproduction) and could therefore also fall into the hands of non-students, he preferred to work out some things in the text itself. Due to this the book has taken on a somewhat hybrid character: the *Remarks* take up much more space than the "more abstract text" of the sections containing the real content of the work.

The second reason for the *Philosophy of Right*'s being a special sort of compendium related back to the description of a compendium given in the third sentence. The common notion (*Vorstellung*) of philosophy sees it as a speaking or writing which must always begin anew and which never comes to an end. Just as the fabric that Penelope unraveled each night, philosophy, too, is a weaving of words which achieves nothing definite due to its always searching for but not finding the right beginning. If this opinion about philosophy is correct, a philosophical compendium is impossible, since a compendium presupposes an agreed-upon content.

The opinion to which Hegel refers here could refer to actual philosophy which, since Descartes, has spent most of its time and energy looking for an uncontestable basis, a primary starting-point, an indubitable principle or absolute foundation. After Kant, many others including Reinhold, Fichte, Schelling and Hegel himself had studied the fundamental question of the true and certain principle of thought and reality. Their everlasting differences, however, even with their own ideas of a year earlier, had to give the public the impression that philosophy knows no certainty but remains forever in doubt and argument. There is nothing to summarize in it because no truths have been ascertained.

Hegel maintains that the truth can indeed be known, and that philosophy is a system of *true* insights. He defends this claim forcefully, not only rhetorically (e.g., in the subsequent parts of the *Preface* and in other introductions) but also and especially in a philosophical way: by developing that system in thinking. True philosophy, then, turns out to be not a discovery on Hegel's part but the result of a very long history of thought, one in which Hegel is the most recent speaker. The history of philosophy is not a chaos which need only be unraveled: it is rather the steady production of a well-constructed fabric which remains hidden from the blind but is visible to true philosophers. The eyes which one must have for it consist in a certain kind of "sight" or "insight". The trivial question of whether this book is a compendium (with which the *Preface* began) thus leads to the question of the proper way of thinking in philosophy, i.e., the question of philosophical method.

Paragraph 3 (p. IV–V)[13]

> I need hardly say that the chief difference between this compendium (*Grundriss*) and an ordinary compendium (*Kompendium*) lies in the method which constitutes its guiding principle. But in this book I am presupposing that philosophy's mode of progression from one topic to another and its mode of scientific proof – this whole speculative way of knowing – is essentially distinct from any other way of knowing. It is only insight into the necessity of such a difference that can rescue philosophy from the shameful decay in which it is immersed at the present time. It is true that the forms and rules of the old logic, of definition, division and syllogism, which include the rules of discursive thinking, (*Verstandeserkenntnis*), have become known as inadequate for speculative science; or rather their inadequacy has not been known; it has only been felt, and then these rules have been thrown off as if they were mere fetters in order to allow the heart, the imagination, and casual intuition to say what they pleased. And since reflection and connexions of thought have after all to come on the scene as well, there is an unconscious relapse into the despised method of commonplace deduction and argumentation (*Räsonnement*).– Since I have fully expounded the nature of speculative knowing in my *Science of Logic*, in this compendium I have only added an explanatory note here and there about procedure and method. In dealing with a topic which is concrete and intrinsically of so varied a character, I have omitted to bring out and demonstrate the chain of logical argument in each and every detail. For one thing, to have done this might have been regarded as superfluous where acquaintance with philosophical method is presupposed; for another, it will be obvious from the work itself that the whole, like the formation of its parts, rests on the logical spirit. It is also from this point of view above all that I should like my book to be taken and judged. What we have to do with here is philosophical *science*, and in such science content is essentially bound up with form.[14]

As opposed to the cited opinion, Hegel maintains that his book is a compendium, in spite of the superficial objection that the *Remarks* already contain a certain working out of the major arguments. The real reason why this compendium is so unusual can be found in the *method* governing it. This is the only true, strictly scientific, and thus philosophical and speculative method, one which is misunderstood and held in contempt by the majority of so-called philosophers.

From the characterization of the style distinguishing Hegel's compendium from other compendia, a transition is made to a polemic which will take up a large part of the preface. The accusation of the "shameful decay" of philosophy "in our time" and the criticism of pseudo-philosophers which follow, however, are at the same time a presentation of the true way of thinking which can still save philosophy.

Hegel does not explain here in a scientific or philosophical fashion how the true method works. An understanding of method can only result from a study of the entire *Science of Logic*, on which he wrote thousands of pages between 1812–1816 and to which he dedicated 191 sections in his *Encylopedia* of 1817.[15] The question of the proper method for philosophy cannot be answered unless one treats the question of the essence and nature of philosophy, but this question is the central one in a metaphilosophical reflection on the formal elements of philosophy.

Concerning the true method, Hegel says here only that it is a scientific progression by means of proofs. With the adjective "speculative" he distinguishes it from two misconceptions concerning the nature of philosophy: 1) traditional logic, which was transmitted by Wolff's scholasticism, i.e., a logic of the intellect's definitions, divisions and reasoning (a *Verstandeslogik*) and 2) a sentimental philosophy which considers itself to be above the logic of the understanding but is unconsciously totally ruled by it. The *Preface* says nothing further about the first misconception; the second, on the other hand, receives Hegel's full attention. It fails not only theoretically, but also – much more so than the philosophy of the intellect – in its practical consequences with relation to right, morality and politics. With the thinking of the intellect (*Verstandesdenken*), it shares its blindness to reason's speculative thinking. But it also falls back, on a lower level than the intellect, to spontaneous and uncontrolled feelings, images, representations, fantasies ("ideas") and opinions. It rejects the rules of the understanding and prefers a vague but emotional and "heartfelt" language to the sharpness of definitions and the discipline of valid syllogisms. Its dislike for all logic is the result of an immature rejection of all rules. As soon as it detects (or feels) a rule, it rebels against these "chains".[16] In so far as the adherents to this "philosophy" do not spout nonsense, their comments are governed and ruled – whether they know or recognize it or not – by the logical relations which logic has correctly distinguished and categorized as the basis of all meaningful speech. They are not better than those thinkers who follow the rules of the intellect, but more unaware and thus worse.

There is something positive in their rejection of traditional logic, in so far as that logic does not reach the level of genuine philosophical or speculative thinking. But their mistake is two-fold. 1) The fact that the intellect's thought is "inadequate" for speculative thinking does not mean that it is superfluous or incorrect. It is only the absolutizing of the intellect and the resulting suppression of the higher thought of reason which produces falsehood. In themselves, the definitions and distinctions produced by the intellect's reflections are useful and necessary. They must however be integrated (and thus transformed) in function of a higher way of thought. 2) The philosophers of the heart base their rejection of the old logic on their feelings. Now in philosophy this dependence on emotion is dangerous. On the one hand, feeling is the most immediate form in which genuine truths make themselves known to us; on the other hand, however, it is not the proper criterion for distinguishing truth from falsehood. Immediate feelings can suggest mistakes as well as truths.[17] Only the intellect and reason together are able to judge the truth (or value) of a feeling. Whoever despises them[18] delivers himself over to an uncontrolled and uncontrollable element and is in fact governed by an unconscious and bad sort of logic.

In the second part of paragraph 3, Hegel briefly indicates what the relation is between this treatise on the philosophy of right and his book on logic. The nature of philosophical thinking, the way in which it is productive, and its method are explained in that book. The philosophy of right is to be the product of a consideration which takes place in accordance with the structures described in the *Logic*. Hegel would have saved us a lot of trouble if he had indicated the logical principles and links on which each section and each transition in the *Philosophy of Right* was based. Every part of the book would then have had a double level: the consideration of a "juridical" point would in each case be accompanied by a meta-theoretical consideration making its logical structure and justification explicit. Except for an "esplanatory note here and there about procedure", however, Hegel has not given such an explication. The reasons he gives for this are the following: a) the subject being discussed here is already extensive enough ("In dealing with a topic which is concrete and intrinsically of so varied a character..."); b) considering the fact that the reader can learn scientific method from my *Science of Logic*, it is superfluous to consider it here as well; c) the reader will see that the entire book and the development of its various sections "is based on the logical spirit". Not one of these arguments is truly convincing. (a) Hegel did not have to worry about increasing the number of pages. He wrote longer and thicker books![19] (b) It is not superfluous, but very instructive and not easy, to show with reference to a concrete theory how it is generated by the abstract method. (c) "The logical spirit" is an unclear expression, in no way identical to a worked-out analysis of the logical moments from which a concrete theory derives its consistency and legitimacy. It seems as though Hegel is excusing himself in a rather clumsy way for a negligence which is much more serious than he lets on. The seriousness of the matter to which he refers does not lie in the scientific or unscientific character of his philosophy of right. Hegel himself insists on this seriousness: as we will see, the entire *Preface* is one long plea for scientific (i.e. philosophical) thinking concerning right and politics. At the end of the *Preface* (par. 20), he again repeats what he said at the end of paragraph 3: this treatise is primarily concerned with scientific or philosophical quality (and not with political position). I do not take seriously any critics who do not see it as a scientific argument (but merely as a political pamphlet) and argue against it with scientific or philosophical means.[20] The entire polemic which follows in paragraph 4 ff. also turns on the question of what a scientific treatment of right and politics involves. And paragraph 3 ends with Hegel's fundamental and often repeated claim that the content of a true science is essentially linked to its form. This means that nothing in science may be claimed unless it is proved in a strictly scientific way, i.e., according to the true method or logic.

In light of the primary importance attributed to logic, it seems strange that Hegel so quickly dismisses the question of whether and to what degree his philosophy of right is actually a concretization of his *Logic*. Although this question concerns the heart of Hegel's system, there have been very few studies done on it until now, and these have not led to any fundamental insight or agreement among the specialists. Here we find practically virgin territory for research. But perhaps Hegel himself already knew how difficult such research is. It is not impossible that he went to work intuitively in writing the *Philosophy of Right*, without constantly taking into consideration the logical structures by means of which he could proceed from one conclusion to the next. Is he referring with "the logical spirit" to such a procedure, in which the mind's eye is directed to a subject (in this case *right*), while an unthematized but implicitly active logic accompanies and rules thematic thought? In that case, making the logical elements in the philosophy of right explicit would have also demanded a great deal of work on Hegel's part. It is not *a priori* certain that the same logic than would have appeared as that presented in the *Science of Logic* (1812–1816), which he had already modified in his *Encylopedia* of 1817.[21]

Paragraph 4 (p. VI–VII)

> We may of course hear from those who seem to be taking a profound view that the form is something external and indifferent to the subject-matter, that the latter alone is important; further, the task of a writer, especially a writer on philosophy, may be said to lie in the discovery of truth, the statement of truth, the dissemination of truth and sound concepts. But if we consider how this task is as a rule actually discharged, what we find in the first place is that the same old stew is continually warmed up again and again and served round to everybody – a task that will even be meritorious in educating and stimulating men's hearts, though it might preferably be regarded as the superfluous labour of a busybody – 'They have Moses and the Prophets, let them hear them'. In particular, we have ample opportunity to marvel at the pretentious tone recognizable in these busybodies when they talk as if the world had wanted for nothing except their energetic dissemination of truths, or as if their *réchauffé* were productive of new and unheard-of truths and was to be specially taken to heart before everything else 'today' and every day. But in this situation we also find one party giving out truths of this sort only to have them dislodged and brushed aside by truths of just the same sort purveyed by other parties. In this press of truths, there is something neither new nor old but perennial; yet how else is this to be lifted out of these reflections which oscillate from this to that without method, how else is it to be separated from them and proved, if not by philosophic science?

The last sentence of paragraph 3 is at the same time an introduction to paragraph 4. In the name of the proper conception of philosophical method, which as the summary of all of philosophy's formal elements can also be called the "form" of philosophy or science, Hegel criticizes an accepted optic which separates the method of science from its content. The optic in question is found not only and not even primarily in the philosophers of feeling against which paragraph 3 and the whole

Preface are directed; it is found in all non-speculative philosophies and is the expression of the thinking of the intellect in the realms of epistemology and logic.

The thesis which is brought into question is: what matters is the "thing" (or the content) of which we speak; the form (i.e., the way in which we formulate and discuss this) is unimportant. It can be beautiful or ugly, concise or sloppy, but it falls outside the realm of truth, i.e., of the matter with which we are concerned. What is said here concerning all written works means the following with respect to philosophy: what matters is the discovery and formulation of *truths*, i.e. a proper understanding of certain matters. The way in which this takes place – by means of which logical and methodological rules – is not important.

It is possible, in a certain sense, to defend the idea that philosophy is concerned with truths. Although it suggests that philosophy is comprised of a multiplicity of truths, it can be understood as an incomplete expression of the insight that the one complete truth is a whole composed of many moments. But the first point at which Hegel directs his attack is not the intellect's fragmentation of the total of truth but the consequences of the separation of content and method for the opponent's search for truth. Precisely *how* that separation corresponds to the actual results of the incriminated philosophy the text does not indicate. *That* there is a connection is stated in Hegel's remark that the form and the content of science are irrevocably bound together. Hegel's argument is thus more rhetorical and *ad hominem* than it is logical or justifiable in terms of his own system. Instead of a refutation of the supposed separation or a positive proof of the unity of form and content (for which we must consult his *Logic*) Hegel says: Look what a mess these fellows make of it! But he does not prove here that the weakness of their philosophy is caused by the above-mentioned separation.

Hegel's first objection is that the philosophers in question have nothing new to offer, but only the "same old stew." There is nothing wrong with re-introducing old truths to the public; on the contrary, it is useful and necessary for the transmission of a culture *via* education and media. The translation and actualization of one's spiritual inheritance is a worthwhile activity. But the best method for doing this is not the "warming up of the same old stew"; it is a return to a critique of the great classics, which Hegel presents by means of a biblical quotation[22] as the ever-modern founders of true science. If one enables others to read the classical texts of philosophy, new treatises which make no new claims but in which old ideas are dished up in a weak and unappetizing fashion become superfluous. Although the contemporary versions of the ancient truths cannot be denied a certain merit, their authors make themselves ridiculous by the tone they assume and the pretention that they have discovered totally new truths which "today" and "in our time" are of the greatest importance. The noise they make praising their own truths is evidence of their ignorance concerning the wisdom of their predecessors, stronger and more tasteful than their own.

Concerning the second objection, which is contained in the last two sentences of the paragraph (beginning with "But in this situation"), it may be seen that there is a clearer relation to the separation of philosophy's form and content than was the case with the former objection, although the relation is not made wholly explicit here either. Since these thinkers consider method to be unimportant, and are therefore unconsciously governed by the traditional method (cf. also par. 3), they have no means of scientifically justifying the "truths" which they propound. It is thus possible to oppose other truths to them, and the end result is a chaos of mutually contradictory statements. Whether those statements are old or new is unimportant; what is important is the question of whether or not they are genuinely *true*, and thus *permanent*, and not limited to earlier or present times. That question, however, can only be solved by a kind of thinking which is considered by science to be methodical or logical. The form is decisive for the rationality and solidity, i.e., the truth, of the content.

Paragraph 5 (p. VII)

> After all, the truth about Right, Ethicity (*Sittlichkeit*)[23] and the State is not only old, but also publicly recognized and formulated by public laws, the public moral standards and religion (*in den öffentlichen Gesetzen, der öffentlichen Moral und Religion offen dargelegt und bekannt*). What more does this truth require – since the thinking mind is not content to possess it in this ready fashion? It requires to be grasped in thought (*begreifen*) as well; the content which is already rational in principle must win the form of rationality and so appear well-founded to free thinking. Such thinking does not remain stationary at the given, whether the given be upheld by

> the external positive authority of the state or the *consensus hominum*, or by the authority of inward feeling and emotion and by the witness of the spirit which directly concurs with it. On the contrary, thought which is free starts out from itself and thereupon claims to know itself as united in its innermost being with the truth.[24]

Through the "after all" which begins this paragraph the text takes a turn in the direction of the major theme of the *Preface*: from this point on it involves not only a scientific discussion on method but also a discussion on the relation of the science (or philosophy) of right to the actuality of right with which it is concerned. Taking his cue from the claim of those believing that truth can only consist in new discoveries, Hegel asserts that the truth concerning right, morality and state is *ancient* and well-known, and that the task of a philosophy of right, morality and state consists not in finding new truths, but in understanding the ancient truth which is already known. The way in which the truth is already familiar to us is a pre-scientific one: it is contained in the existing legal order ("the laws"), the presently functioning morality and the accepted religion by which public life is governed.

What Hegel asserts here is shocking, certainly at first sight. Is he not preaching a pure conservativism of the established order? Or is he a flatterer who does not dare to say what he thinks? The censors can be satisfied: this book appears to take the side of the Prussian government against the critical students and professors, defending law and order by means of dismissals and censorship.

An interpretation of this and the following ambiguous paragraphs is only possible on the basis of an insight into others of Hegel's texts, texts which were not written under the influence of political developments or as a part of a political position and which therefore have a more scientific and less rhetorical character. Concerning the problems touched on and presupposed by this paragraph, the following ideas appear (in reading other texts) to be constant elements of Hegel's system:

a) Philosophy constructs its truth not on the basis of an abstract principle but through an analysis and synthesis of the concrete actuality, which it first gets to know as a given here and now through some form of immediate experience. Hegel's speculative thought is not less empirical than that of Locke or Hume, but it is more concrete. It is not limited to the illumination of abstract aspects of the givens (*dem Gegebenen*) which present themselves, but attempts to include all of the factually empirical in its concept.[25]

b) With reference to cultural realities such as right, morality, art and religion, this "empiricism" in Hegel's philosophy means that it proceeds from the factual reality of these cultural realities here and now. The first acquaintance with right, ethics, religion and so on, one which is decisive for the aftermath, takes place through the education which teaches us in a authoritarian way what people, i.e., the existing culture, think and do about them. By taking part in our culture we have a living experience of it, one not yet rationally justified. Right, ethics and religion are not the products of any one individual who just thinks them up. Just as is the case with language, they have existed from time immemorial and have shaped themselves into what is now the culture of our society.[26]

c) The task of philosophy does not consist in the creation of a good legal system or a true religion out of nothing or nearly nothing; it consists in understanding the "present incarnate" (*leibhaftige Gegenwart*, cf. Husserl) which confronts it *via* experience. Philosophy is not the designing of Utopias (which in fact are necessarily the products and transformations of actually experienced realities), but the attempt to acquire insight into the existing actuality and to justify it to reason.[27]

d) The factual existence of certain cultural realities is not yet a proof of their correctness, value or "truth". In every culture there must also be a certain degree of criticism concerning the characteristic values, conceptions and attitudes of that culture. Hegel's work is no mere translation of the existing order into the language of the intellect, it is also a criticism of that order, in which many aspects of its habitual science, morality, philosophy, religion, politics and legal institutions are negatively judged.[28]

e) The critique, however, cannot include the whole of the culture in all of its aspects. The factual existence of right, rationality, art and religion and the transformations they have undergone in the course of their histories (e.g., through their self-criticism) can be complete nonsense ("untruth"). At the root of philosophy lies the conviction that the existing culture is governed by a certain fundamental rationality, just as is nature (cf. par. 7), and that the actuality of the universe as it is or has become, in fact is intelligible, at least for the most part.[29]

f) Hegel's belief in the (at least overall) rationality of actuality is expressed in a philosophy of culture (called "philosophy of the objective and absolute spirit"[30]) which attempts to understand the factuality of existing religion, art, state, morality and so on but is hampered in doing so by improper conditions and phenomena which can only be understood as distortions, absolutizations, imperfect preliminary stages or corrupt forms of the genuine truth which is actualized in them. The rationality (or truth) and irrationality (or untruth; falsehood) of the world of spirit must be understood within the framework of history, in which spirit actualizes itself only gradually and *via* various stages. To the extent that the factual culture is not meaningless it has an actual truth; to the extent that it is not yet completely rational it represents not the final point of the development in which spirit realizes itself *in concreto* but a temporary stage in which there is room for improvement.[31]

In light of the ideas summarized here the peculiar statements in paragraph 5 can be better understood.

The first two sentences suggest that the *entire* truth concerning right, morality and state (i.e., the entire content of the *Philosophy of Right*) has already been recognized and expressed in a pre-philosophical but trustworthy way, *viz.*, in the positive laws and widely accepted morality and religion of the existing state. The commandments and laws of the existing legal order, morality and religion are already "in themselves" considered to form a "rational content". Philosophy should need only to translate this content into the form of logical justification.

Hegel's remark that the truth of the existing legal order is "old" shows that by this "truth" he cannot mean the whole of the Prussian legal order around 1820. Since the time of the French Revolution and Napoleon much had changed, not only in the legal codes governing the societies of Prussian and other German and European lands but also in the praxis of social and political life.[32] The truth of public laws, morality and religion is only old in so far as a greater or smaller core of them had already been realized earlier – before 1815? before Napoleon? before 1789? even earlier? In any case Hegel *cannot* mean here that the truth about right simply coincides with the factual regulations and institutions existing in 1820. Besides this we must realize that it is far from clear what is meant by "the public morality and religion". Was there only one morality and religion? This can only be maintained if one takes morality and religion in a very global sense. Hegel was well aware of the fact that the culture of 1820 was a battlefield of moral and religious ideas, and his polemics, in particular against a number of powerful contemporary theologians, is evidence of this. "The public laws" were also extremely various depending on whether one was thinking of Prussia, France, England or some other German land.

The first proof that Hegel could not mean that the whole truth concerning right has been realized in the existing laws and order, consists in the systematic unfolding of right which makes up the (according to him only true) content of the *Philosophy of Right*. Not only does Hegel criticize 19th century civil society for not alleviating the poverty and misery into which it forces a large number of the population,[33] he also develops a system of public law which differs in crucial respects from all of the states existing in 1820. Many of its elements can be found in the progressive Prussia of immediately after 1815, but various other elements which Hegel deduced (and which as deduced are the only rational and true aspects of state) elements, such as bi-cameral popular representation, public debates in the various houses containing representatives of various classes and trial by jury, did not exist there.[34]

If Hegel could not mean that philosophy has only to understand and justify what is prescribed by the existing order of right, morality and religion, why then does he write things which almost must mislead an unprepared reader? Did he fall subject to the emotions which belong to polemic? Although Hegel is sometimes vehement and gruff, he does not give impression of being an impassioned author. There must be a special reason for the ambiguity which, certainly in the political situation after Kotzebue's death (March 23, 1819), could only lead to misunderstandings. Did Hegel write this *Preface* (or this part – the beginning – of the *Preface*) primarily with an eye on the censors and/or government? If his book was meant not only for students and colleagues but also to influence the politics of Prussia's government, as his letter to Hardenberg makes us suspect,[35] he perhaps wanted to win the benevolence of those in power by giving them the impression in the *Preface* that he was on their side. Then his *Preface* would primarily be a political and strategic work, with which he intended to mobilize power rather than insight. But this intention contradicts that formulated in paragraphs 3 and 20 as his primary or even sole intention, *viz.*, that his book is not a polemic but a scientific work, as which it must be judged. Even if Hegel did not consciously play the role of sycophant so sharply criticized by Plato,[36] his book was as little successful as Plato's *Republic* in achieving its wished for result: Hegel's scientific colleagues, as well as the general public, condemned it as evidence of reactionary tendencies and not as a scientific argument. The government was not very impressed by the book in either direction.[37]

The second half of paragraph 5 forms a counter-balance to the first half, which seemed so accommodating to the established order. If philosophy consists in the understanding of a content that is already actual and rational (and not in creating dreams and other Utopia's), it realizes in that undertaking a *liberation*. As the acquisition of insight and the justification of facts and givens that initially seem opaque and merely posited or "positive", thinking liberates. And *vice versa*: because a human being is a thinking and free being, he or she cannot be satisfied at the level of spontaneous experience and the acceptance of things and rules which just happen to be one way and not another. One's first and immediate acquaintance with reality is a naive subjection to an external authority. The phenomena simply impose themselves on the observer: "Thou shalt not kill", "God created us." With the awakening of the intellect, the obviousness of this acceptance disappears, and the question arises of whether the content previously believed or experienced is indeed true. A distant, critical phase of primarily negative reactions begins a trial during which the thinking person tries to ascertain the inner plausibility of theses previously accepted on authority. The authority belonging to immediate knowledge gives way to a knowledge which can account for itself by giving and connecting various reasons:[38] this is rational knowledge or a concept.

The authority on which our initial or immediate knowledge of right, etc. is based is differentiated in the last sentence of paragraph 5 into three kinds. Something can be a given a) by its being posited by the external authority of the state (e.g., in the form of state-imposed or "positive" laws); b) by the fact that all or almost all people agree that it is or ought to be so; c) by our being told it is so by an inner "voice" which comes from our feelings, heart or spirit. From this summary we can deduce several important insights.

By Hegel's comparing the external authority of the state to the inner voice of our feelings and the immediate evidence of our spirit (the latter expression is used primarily in a religious context[39]) he contests the claim of those who believe that an appeal to their feelings or heart frees their thinking and safeguards it from subjection to the authority which other citizens and believers cannot or may not avoid. This kind of revolutionary is just as subject to an authority as are those others. They let themselves be carried off by their enthusiasm without testing its quality. Only thinking – i.e., a conceptual insight – can free us from naïveté and both external and internal dependence on positive powers. Enthusiasm is no proof of correctness. Even if truth and values do initially (and later) present themselves in the form of a feeling, as Hegel often affirms, the untrue and evil do this as well. Feeling itself is not suited to functioning as a criterion; it must be evaluated and approved by a higher authority – by reason and the intellect.

The second form of authority or positivity which Hegel names here is the famous *consensus gentium*, to which not only philosophers but also theologians of the seventeenth and eighteenth centuries liked to appeal.[40] Hegel refers to this many times in relation to the so-called "proofs for the existence of God"[41] and makes clear in those contexts that an agreement of opinions is *not* a criterion for their truth. In fact this is easy to see if we consider that truth is not a given or observable fact but something possessing a universal validity. Only if one could show that the *factual* universality of an opinion could not be explained otherwise than as the expression or effect of a truth that is also shown in that opinion would consensus be an indication of a true content. According to Hegel's way of thinking one would then still have to show how that truth in itself exists, and how it fits together with all other truths, for a true content without the true form of the concept is still a doxa, as Plato would say: more surface than the truth itself.

The state's authority, which is expressed among other ways by "public laws" and which protects and advances "public morality and religion", is compared at the end of paragraph 5 with two other forms of given and fallible authority. There is a good chance that the censor, after the paragraph's pleasing first sentence, will read over this comparison. But there is an implicit statement that the state's authority is just as little a criterion for the truth concerning right, morality and state as is spontaneous feeling, the authority of which will be ridiculed in the following sections even more vehemently than was done in paragraph 3. Even if Hegel wanted to say in the first sentence that there is a true core within the factual legal order, morality and religion, he at any rate does not state that that core is true *because* it is imposed or protected by the state. On the contrary: if the state's authority is reliable (and the same is true for consensus and the inner voice of feeling and conscience), this is the result of the truth itself, i.e., ultimately of the spirit which has made itself known in this authority thanks to an entire history of development, full of strife and defeats. A positive fact cannot ground a single truth; rather, the truth of a positive fact is justified by reason. This justification consists in understanding, which elevates the form of the given and the authority with which it imposes itself on us to the scientific and free form of the concept. This occurs when thinking does not remain a mere internal occurrence but discovers the core of the given confronting it and unites itself to it by an insight. The freedom of this thinking is not a subjection to some sort of external or internal authority, but it does not remain a protest against everything positive either. Concrete freedom is the recognition or the inner quality and truth of things and the becoming one with the spirit at work in them.

Paragraph 6 (p. VII–VIII)

> The unsophisticated heart takes the simple line of adhering with trustful conviction to the publicly accepted truth and then building on this firm foundation its conduct and its set position in life. Against this simple line of conduct there may at once be raised the alleged difficulty of how it is possible, in an infinite variety of opinions, to distinguish and discover what is universally recognized and valid (*Gültige*). This perplexity may at first sight be taken for a right and really serious attitude to the thing (*die Sache*), but in fact those who boast of this perplexity are in the position of not being able to see the wood for the trees; the only perplexity and difficulty they are in is one of their own making. Indeed, this perplexity and difficulty of theirs is proof rather that they want as the substance of the right and the ethical not what is universally recognized and maintained (*geltende*), but something else. If they had been serious with what is universally accepted instead of busying themselves with the vanity and particularity of opinions and things, they would have clung to what is substantively right, namely to the commands of the ethical order and the state, and would have regulated their lives in accordance with these. – A more serious difficulty arises, however,

> from the fact that man thinks and tries to find in thinking both his freedom and the basis of ethicity. But however lofty, however divine, this right [of thought] may be, it is perverted into wrong if it is only this [opining] which passes for thinking and if thinking knows itself to be free only when it diverges from what is *universally* recognized and valid and when it has discovered how to invent for itself something *particular*.[42]

A source of many difficulties and discussions concerning the *Preface* is the fact that Hegel constantly refuses to clarify the ambiguity of what is presented there by drawing sharp distinctions. The literary genre he is employing even seems to require this ambiguity.

The following sections maintain the suggestion, made in paragraph 5, that what is positively given coincides with "the ancient truth" and that the factually valid laws, morality and religion are the immediate and "most familiar" way in which the (genuine) truth of right, morality and state imposes itself. Paragraph 6 draws no distinction between "the universally recognized and valid" (*das allgemein Anerkannte und Gültige*) and "the universally recognized and maintained" (*das allgemein Anerkannte und Geltende*). The practised (*geltende*) and universally accepted "commands of the ethical order and the state" are simply equated to "the matter" (*die Sache*, Knox: "*the thing*"), "the substance of the right and the ethical" (*die Substanz des Rechten und Sittlichen*), "the substantively right" (*das substantielle Recht*), and opposed to "the vanity and particularity of opinion" (*die Eitelkeit und Besonderkeit des Meinens*), which is expressed in deviations from the universally valid and accepted. The identification of the accepted and the valid which Hegel makes here can – as said – at most be made with reference to part, perhaps the core, of the factual condition of right and morality. As can be seen in Hegel's *Philosophy of World History*, but also in sections and *Remarks* contained in the *Philosophy of Right*,[43] the non-identity of fact and truth was a constant characteristic of the political systems and cultures of which our past is comprised. If Hegel means that the situation of right and state in 1820 corresponds globally to the truth of "the matter" in question – if he considers the modern state, of which Prussia is a progressive example, to be a proper realisation of juridical and ethical "substance" – he must prove this opinion somehow by showing that the true concept of that substance is recognizable in the factuality of what is positively given. The *Preface* necessarily appeals to the proof in which the book consists. To evaluate

Hegel's claim, an analysis of the entire work and a historical reconstruction of the situation in 1820 are essential. But in reading the *Philosophy of Right* we find again and again that Hegel obfuscates the difference between the idea or truth of right and the factual situation of the given and legal system. This is particularly the case where he polemizes against critics and moralists who appeal to their heart or feeling or conscience to condemn the existing political reality.

The opposition we find predominating in paragraph 6 is that of "simple", naive, and "unprejudiced" *trust*[44] concerning the universally accepted order of right and morality on the one hand, and various, especially incorrect ways of thinking on the other. As was said in paragraph 5, one *cannot* be satisfied with a naive acceptance: we must examine their legitimacy and the foundations on which they are based. The necessity of doing this is at the same time a right, for it is an expression as well, as a realisation of human freedom.[45] But this right becomes injustice – it is distorted, does not lead to freedom and is therefore no longer a right – when thinking is exercised in a particular, irrational and unfree way.

In the incorrect way of thinking which Hegel criticizes here he sees an expression of particularism and vanity. Not every error in thought constitutes an injustice, but thinking which basically consists in rejecting universality must hate all legality, and thus the quintessence or "substance" of right and morality.[46] Just as all thinking, it begins with a naive trust, but it then loses itself in endless discussions on all sorts of opinions concerning the composition, needs and obligations of right and morality. The forest (substance, core and foundation) of right disappears from our field of vision due to our busying ourselves with the many trees: *viz.* the multiplicity of various opinions which are all taken seriously – more seriously than the universally recognized and universally accepted truth which can form a solid basis for life and action.

In itself, of course, there is nothing wrong with a philosopher's analyzing and discussing the many and various opinions concerning right and morality. The question of how to find a solid point of reference in the chaos of opinions is a serious problem for every philosopher, and it is no disgrace if someone cannot solve this "perplexity and difficulty" once and for all. But this discussion takes a wrong turn as soon as its intention is directed away from the discovery of the core and foundation of right and politics – which make a universally valid order possible – and concentrates on the particular vision which one holds as opposed to others and especially to the universally accepted institutions. This penchant for the individual, this particularism arising out of vanity, betrays itself according to Hegel in a contempt for the universally accepted and maintained order, or, as it is formulated in paragraph 9, in "hatred of law". The error does not lie in the concern with the individual but in the rejection of the universal, which results in the absolutization and insolubility of individual opinions. The misconception of the truth which Hegel denounces here is attended by an illusion concerning freedom: one thinks one makes oneself free by deviating from the universal. Protest and "originality" are considered to be the distinguishing characteristics of freedom. This particularism is however such a fundamental error that it makes every philosophy of right impossible.

The rhetorical schema in which Hegel polemizes here and elsewhere sets up an opposition between the conceptual *universal* in the form of the factually universal and the *particular* in the form of its absolutization by vanity (or elsewhere: by another form of subjectivism and egoism).[47]

In the true concept, universality and individuality are united as two moments within one particular. But this unity differs from a naïve lack of differentiation due to the understanding's differentiating and analysing the universal and the particular before their synthesis is comprehended by reason. It is necessary to make the particular relatively independent, but this is only a stage on the way to the (also universal) unity in which the moments that were already present from the beginning in a confused unity are now taken up in a conceptual fashion.[48]

It is thus certainly not true that a discussion concerning the difficulty of finding a way out of the chaos of opinions is *ipso facto* suspect if it encounters a certain difficulty in achieving its object. That difficulty is real and not, as Hegel says, merely "alleged". But the absolutization of the viewpoint which only considers the particular (for example in the form of priding oneself on one's own opinion, sketched in paragraph 6) does not do justice to the universal aspect of the actuality with which it deals. The same must be said, *mutatis mutandis*, of an absolutization despising, forgetting or ridiculing those particular aspects or opinions as such, and it is not right that the "perplexity and difficulty" pointed out should itself be considered a "proof" of a certain disdain for the universally accepted. The network of distinctions made by the intellect and the battle of particular opinions are essential parts of philosophy, but if the core ("the substance") holding all of this together is lost in their midst, those particularities lose their truth.

With this argumentation Hegel can only attack a philosophy which has no understanding of universality, synthesis and totality. But *nothing* can be proved by it concerning the question of whether the universal, the synthesis of the concept, the true synthesis or totality is in fact realized here and now. A Utopian or alternative vision of right, morality and state, one which considers these themes as articulations of an organic unity, but criticizes existing reality in light of the unity of universality and particularity and rejects it on fundamental grounds, is immune to the line of argumentation presented above. When Hegel's opponents protest the Prussian state organization or the Karlsbad resolutions due to their inability to find a rationally justifiable totality in them, their criterion is correct, even if their thinking is perhaps insufficient. On the other hand, due to his desire to find peace with the political actuality,[49] Hegel could be running the risk of viewing it too optimistically and thus of interpreting it as a satisfactory system when this is not the case. The question of the relation between the thought (i.e., the comprehended idea) on the one hand, and the factual existence of right here and now on the other, must be clearly distinguished from the question of the relation between the universal and the particular as elements of the concept of the true idea (realized in fact or not). The unity of the universal and the particular is proved by the (onto-) logic of the concept; the unity of the true idea and factual existence is a problem which can not be solved by a mere (onto-)logical development. Besides a logic of essence,[50] this would also demand a philosophy of history and of the here and now. One of the rhetorical elements which make the *Preface* so difficult is the amalgam of the questions distinguished and the suggestion that an answer to one question also implies an answer to the other.

If by his reference to the universally maintained and accepted institutions Hegel intends to do anything other than flatter the government or provide evidence of his subjective satisfaction with the existing "law and order", he owes us a proof of his subjective insurance and individual opinion. In any case his appeal to the structure of the true concept is insufficient for providing the complaint made in paragraph 5 with a rational foundation. If the proof asked for is provided by him elsewhere, that will still stupport the accusations he makes here. But if further study shows that he always presupposes that "truth" of the existing situation which he must prove, the rhetoric of this *Preface* is symptomatic of the fact that his satisfaction rests on a "trustful conviction" which probably cannot be justified.

Paragraph 7 (p. VIII–X)

> At the present time, the idea that freedom of thought, and of spirit generally, evinces itself only in divergence from, indeed in hostility to, what is publicly recognized, might seem to be most firmly rooted in connexion with the state, and it is chiefly for this reason that a philosophy of the state might seem essentially to have the task of discovering and promulgating still another theory, and a new and particular one at that. In examining this idea and the activity in conformity with it, we might suppose that no state or constitution had ever existed in the world at all or was even in being at the present time, but that nowadays – and this 'nowadays' lasts for ever – we had to start all over again from the beginning, and that the ethical world had just been waiting for such present-day projects, proofs, and investigations. So far as nature is concerned, people grant that it is nature as it is which philosophy has to bring within its ken, that the philosopher's stone lies concealed somewhere, somewhere within nature itself, that nature is inherently rational, and that what knowledge has to investigate and grasp in concepts is this actual reason present in it; not the formations and accidents evident to the superficial observer, but nature's eternal harmony, its harmony, however, in the sense of the law and essence immanent within it. The ethical world, on the other hand, the state (i.e. reason as it actualizes itself in the element of self-consciousness), is not allowed to enjoy the good fortune which springs from the fact that it is reason which has achieved power and mastery within that element and which maintains itself and has its home there. The universe of spirit is supposed rather to be left to the mercy of chance and caprice (*dem Zufall und der Willkür preisgeben*), to be God-forsaken, and the result of this atheism of the ethical world is that truth lies outside it, and at the same time, since even so reason is supposed to be in it as well, truth becomes nothing but a problem. But it is this also that is to authorize, nay to oblige, every thinker to take his own road, though not in search of the philosopher's stone, for he is saved this search by the philosophizing of our contemporaries, and everyone nowadays is assured that he has this stone in his grasp as his birthright. Now admittedly it is the case that those who live their lives in the state as it actually exists here and now and find satisfaction there for their knowledge and volition (and of these there are many, more in fact than think or know it, because ultimately this

> is the position of everybody), or those at any rate who *consciously* find their satisfaction in the state, laugh at these operations and affirmations and regard them as an empty game, sometimes rather funny, sometimes rather serious, now amusing, now dangerous. Thus this restless activity of vain reflection, together with its popularity and the welcome it has received, would be a thing on its own, developing in privacy in its own way, were it not that it is philosophy itself which has earned all kinds of scorn and discredit by its indulgence in this occupation. The worst of these kinds of scorn is this, that, as I said just now, everyone is convinced that his mere birthright puts him in a position to pass judgement on philosophy in general and to criticize it. No other art or science is subjected to this last degree of scorn, to the supposition that we are masters of it without ado.[51]

What Hegel had said in paragraph 6 concerning the nature of free thinking is now applied to the theory of ethicity (*Sittlichkeit*). To think is to think independently: philosophy is freedom expressing itself in the form of insights. To be free implies a certain distance with reference to the factual situation and to theories which arise. Naive trust in what exists gives way to an attempt at insightful and thus convincing justification. As long as this attempt is unsuccessful, the justification remains problematic and the distance between thinking and the facts is not bridged. This lack of reconciliation can be due to thought as well as to the facts. An insufficient capacity to think or an incorrect method makes insight into the rationality of a rational reality impossible. But it can also be the case that the existing reality is wrong, so that thinking is the last thing that could justify it. Hegel gives examples in several places of this latter kind of short circuit between fact and thought. But they almost always refer to former or non-German realities.[52] One of the possible reactions to an unsatisfactory reality is for consciousness to turn away from it and retreat inward. Thus in the *Remark* to section 138 Hegel refers to Socrates and the Stoics as representatives of a way of thinking which is *unable* to find the true right in existing reality and which therefore seeks it in itself "in ideal inwardness". History has seen many "epochs in which that which is considered to be right and good in reality and morals *cannot* satisfy the *better* will" (my italics). Socrates' will and his conception of right and morality were better than the existing order of right and morality (but they were not more powerful and were thus in a certain sense unreal). In the time of Socrates and the Stoics "the generally accepted duties" (and thus the accepted laws and "commands of the ethical order and the state"), and that which is "universally recognized and maintained (*geltende*)" (of which Hegel speaks in the sixth paragraph of the *Preface*) no longer corresponded with reason's demands. "The existing world of freedom", the universally accepted and "maintained", was *not* identical to the universally "*valid*" (cf. par. 6): the harmony demanded by reason – the *idea* of right and morality – was lost in "actuality" (*Wirklichkeit*). In this kind of situation the thinker *must* retreat inward and "attempt to find the harmony lost in actuality in ideal inwardness *alone*" (*Grl.* 138A).

Hegel is well aware of the fact – personally experienced in his youth – that a "deviation" (*Abweichung*) in thought from what is "publicly recognized" *can* be the expression of a genuine, albeit unhappy, consciousness, one which is justifiably "severed" (*entzweit*)[53] from actuality. In certain periods criticism is the only possible form of philosophy. Nothing can be said *a priori* about the time at which a situation arises in which a philosopher can only be true by dissenting. Ontological principles, a universal belief in providence or the conviction that reason is strong enough to be victorious do not answer the question of whether our current factual situation is in agreement with reason. Even if one believes or knows for certain that the universe and history as a whole are rational, one still does not know *a priori* the degree to which the present situation realizes what history as a whole (if this word means anything) and the *entire* actuality make actual.

We must keep this all in mind in reading Hegel's massive attack on certain critics of the political system that he wants to understand as a rational actuality in the *Philosophy of Right.* Although Hegel does not do much in this *Preface* to draw the distinctions necessary to clearly pointing out his targets, he does not primarily accuse these critics of criticizing the actual state in function of a divergent idea of state and politics, but rather of identifying political philosophy and negative criticism. One would have to further examine whether this characterization of the people Hegel has in mind is justified – it is probably a caricature which should be understood rhetorically (and not morally) – but in any case he does make clear that free thinking on the part of philosophy cannot consist in attempting to think differently than the factual situation suggests come what may. Negations, dissidence and hostility are at the best phases of a process in which, in some way or other, thought and actuality must and shall be reconciled. The idea that everything which exists and everything thought up to now could be worthless, so that we would have to start here and now to think up, ground and construct a system of right and state, reveals a misconception concerning the nature and meaning of history and culture. Just as little as language and morality (for example) still need to be thought up is the state something rooted in a theory abstracting from the centuries-long process through which it has evolved. The critics' fundamental error is that they have more faith in their own subjective "thinking" than they do in the historical reason of spirit which is realized in history. The current order of right, morality and politics is the result of the history of the ethical order as it has taken place up to now. If one believes that this order can only be negatively evaluated, this means that the entire preceding history has had no positive result. But this does not fit together with the notion that the history of humanity and its cultures is guided, at least in certain respects, by a rational "power", principle, spirit or "God".

Within the framework of his "non-esoteric" prefaces directed to a not exclusively philosophical public, and especially with reference to the theologians at whom he is aiming, Hegel often uses religious language in order to portray his opponents as non-believers as well as unscientific theoreticians. Through their opinion that true right must still be discovered they express their conviction that the world of spirit (the objective moment of which is formed by right, morality and the ethical order) is a-rational and the history of the spiritual world a mere product of chance and caprice. If they are right, this would mean that history and the world of spirit are not guided by divine providence. As far as "the ethical world" is concerned, these critics, including the theologians among them, are atheists.

This "atheism of the ethical world", however, contradicts a general conviction which is found also on the part of those critics, *viz.*, that the realm of (non-spiritual) nature is indeed a rational actuality, ruled by laws and necessity and fundamentally well-ordered. Whoever is enough of a philosopher and thinker to see beyond contingencies and superficial "forms" will discover what everyone assumes without any examination at all: nature is a rational actuality. Reason can discover this rationality in the form of universal laws and necessary structures – thus making the natural sciences possible – and need only be open to nature's "eternal harmony" and "immanent law and essence" to do so. In other words, reason need not change or construct nature in order to discover its rationality.

Hegel's argument does not say so explicitly, but it does suggest that if nature is essentially rational, one should *a fortiori* posit the rationality of "the spiritual universe" and thus also of "the ethical world". Here, as elsewhere, Hegel identifies "the ethical world" with "the state"[54] (incorrectly, as we will see), defining the latter as "reason as it actualizes itself in the element of self-consciousness" (*Selbstbewusstsein*). The explanation of this formula cannot yet be given here, but it is clear that it presupposes what ought to be proved against the critics: the state is reason (or rationality) actualized. Even if one denies this, one could still recognize the fact that "self-consciousness" is the element in which the state consists, the building blocks, as it were, out of which it is constructed – that is, if one understands "self-consciousness" as Hegel more properly defines it in the *Introduction* to the *Philosophy of Right*: as the human free will that wills, determines, objectifies and organizes itself. By presenting the state as an actuality of reason and self-consciousness, Hegel suggests that the state, even moreso than nature, must be conceived of as a rational actuality, and that a scientific study of the state must not change it but understand it. It is also true of the state, as it is with nature, that under its superficial forms and contingencies, its motley exterior (*der bunten Rinde*) as it is formulated in paragraph 13, it is a harmony, the "immanent law and essence" of which (par. 7), as its "core" or "heart" and "inner pulse" (par. 13), is to be found by theory. In ethical institutions, Reason (which we may capitalize since it is a super-individual force) has effectuated and validated itself. It lives within them and is a power (*Gewalt*).

Although the negative theories cannot discover anything rational in the state "as it is",[55] they cannot cease to look for the state's rationality, i.e., its truth, since they would then no longer be theories but merely the affirmations of irrationality and contingency. Since the existing state is bad, according to these theories, its truth must exist outside factual existence. The true rationality of the state is something which *ought* to be realized and which must first be sought after (above or beyond the realized state, for example in a theory or Utopia). The true, rational state is not a reality, but a task to be accomplished. The true is "nothing but a problem."[56]

Because the critics feel that true morality has not yet been realized, they believe that thinking about morality primarily means inventing a plan for a good state which would afterwards have to be translated into reality. The primary requirement for the execution of this task is the discovery of a good approach (the philosopher's stone) and method. The theoreticians whom Hegel criticizes here, however, are too naive and too hard-headed to *search for* the key to truth; they presuppose that everyone simply has that key. But science and philosophy have to be learned. Their presupposition is an indication of a contempt for both.

The critical reflection of the naive and hard-headed stands in contrast to the satisfaction of wiser individuals who are aware that the state is not so bad. "Ultimately" (i.e., at the essential level which lies hidden beneath the surface of contingencies) *all* citizens are really satisfied.

The fundamental consensus of all citizens which Hegel is claiming here is justified in the explanation of the ethical reality which comprises the content of the *Philosophy of Right.*[57] Here and elsewhere Hegel expresses his conviction that the juridical, moral and political reality of the world in 1820 is fundamentally satisfactory and that it does justice to the essence of man and humanity (or rationality). Not everyone is *conscious* of this radical agreement between reason and actuality at the level of the state, but that is due to short-sightedness or vanity or some other problem with the critic's attitude. Those who are aware of the agreement – Hegel is probably thinking here not only of philosophers but also of other sensible citizens and especially of politicians – those who are consciously satisfied, react to the criticism of the others with a mixture of irony and disquiet. Since the critical theories do not touch the heart of the matter (if they did, they would no longer be negative), they remain a superficial game, which can be amusedly or ironically observed, just as the reactions they occasion (e.g., the enthusiasm of the fraternities for such theoreticians, but also the political measures affecting them). Although this game can be dangerous, *viz.*, when the dissatisfaction of large groups is too agitated by it, philosophy can consider its development and the reactions to it as a matter with which it does not need to bother and which – *if* it becomes too dangerous – falls under the government's domain.[58]

But there is one respect in which "critical theory" shows its regard for philosophy. By the critics' pose as philosophers and their blurring of the distinction between their reflection and the true science of right and morality, they bring philosophy into discredit. Not only does this have consequences for the public appreciation of philosophy (perhaps Hegel already has in mind here the dictum which he quotes in a note to paragraph 11 (p. XVII), in which doing philosophy is equated to visiting a brothel), it also endangers genuine philosophers: because the government cannot so easily distinguish the genuine from the false, it can easily fall into suspecting the good and basically satisfied philosophers of a revolutionary intention or into a misunderstanding of their statements.

Hegel's characterization of critical theory as a quasi-philosophy reminds one of Plato's distinction between the sophists who are not concerned with truth but with the "motley exterior" (par. 13) of superficial appearance, and philosophers, who are guided by the *ousia* (the essence) and the truth of reality (par. 13). It is even possible that Hegel's statement that "the true" is "nothing but a problem" for his opponents is an allusion to the passage from Plato's *Sophist*, in which Theaetetus characterizes the sophist as being "fruitful in problems".[59] In the context of the *Preface*, the distinction Hegel makes here between the true philosophers who illuminate the rational core and truth of reality and the idle thinkers who criticize everything on the basis of an unscientific reflection which anyone can accomplish has a methodological as well as a political function: Hegel wants to remove true philosophy from the discredit into which those who despise it have brought it.

Paragraph 8 (p. X–XIII)

> In fact, what we have seen recent philosophical publications proclaiming with the maximum of pretension about the state has really justified anybody who cared to busy himself with the subject in this conviction that he could manufacture a philosophy of this kind himself without ado and so give himself proof of his possession of philosophy. Besides, this self-styled 'philosophy' has expressly stated that 'truth itself cannot be known', that that only is true which each individual allows to rise out of his heart, emotion, and inspiration about ethical topics, especially about the state, the government, and the constitution. In this connexion what a lot of flattery has been talked, especially to the young! Certainly the young have listened to it willingly enough. 'He giveth to his own in sleep' has been applied to science and hence every sleeper has numbered himself among "his own", but the concepts he has acquired in sleep are themselves of course only the wares

of sleep. – A ringleader of these hosts of superficiality, of these self-styled 'philosophers', Herr Fries,* did not blush, on the occasion of a public festival which has become notorious, to express the following ideas in a speech on the state and its constitution: 'In the people ruled by a genuine communal spirit, life for the discharge of all public business would come from below, from the people itself; living associations, indissolubly united by the holy chain of friendship, would be dedicated to every single project of popular education and popular service', and so on. – This is the quintessence of shallow thinking, to base [philosophic] science not on the development of thought and the concept but rather on immediate perception (*Wahrnehmung*) and the play of fancy (*die zufällige Einbildung*); to take the rich inward articulation of the ethical, i.e., the state, the architectonic of its rationality – which sets determinate limits to the different circles of public life and their rights, uses the strict accuracy of measurement which holds together every pillar, arch, and buttress and thereby produces the strength of the whole out of the harmony of the parts – to take this structure and confound the completed fabric in the broth of 'heart, friendship, and inspiration'. According to a view of this kind (akin to Epicurus' view on the contingency of the world in general), the world of ethics should be given over – as in fact of course it is not – to the subjective contingency (*Zufälligkeit*) of opinion and caprice (*Willkür*). By the simple family remedy of ascribing to feeling the labour, the more than millenary labour, of reason and its intellect, all the trouble of rational insight and knowledge directed by conceptual thinking is of course saved. On this point, Goethe's Mephistopheles, a good authority!, says something like this, a quotation I have used elsewhere already:

Do but despise intellect and science,
the highest of all man's gifts,
and thou hast surrendered thyself to the devil
and to perdition art doomed.

The next thing is that such sentiments assume even the guise of piety, for this bustling activity has used any and every expedient in its endeavour to give itself authority. With godliness and the Bible, however, it has arrogated to itself the highest of justifications for despising the ethical order and the objectivity of law, since it is piety too which envelops in the simpler intuition of feeling the truth which is articulated in the world into an organic realm. But if it is piety of the right sort, it sheds the form of this [emotional] region so soon as it leaves the inner life, enters upon the daylight of the Idea's development and revealed riches, and brings with it, out of its inner worship of God, reverence for an absolute truth exalted above the subjective form of feeling and for [objective] laws.[60]

* I have borne witness before to the superficiality of his philosophy – see *Science of Logic* (Nuremberg, 1812), Introduction, p. xvii.

The last sentence of paragraph 7 is the prelude to paragraph 8: the notion of philosophy held by the opponent identifies it with a superficial reflection which is "no art"; understood in this way, anyone could do philosophy.

Paragraph 8 begins with a confirmation of the fact that the part of recent political philosophy[61] receiving the most attention is indeed a "philosophy" of the man in the street: everyone can philosophize in this way. This "naïveté which calls itself philosophy" legitimizes itself – and thereby gives everyone the right to call him or herself a philosopher – by a theory of truth that calls every expression of the heart, soul and emotion "true" on the basis of a scepticism concerning objective truth. Every conviction that comes from within is good; the criterion of truth is purely subjective: enthusiasm is sufficient.

A welcome theory for all those who wish to spare themselves the trouble of study! Especially for the youth (students and members of the fraternities) but also for all those unhindered by a consciousness of true problems. The fact that Hegel quotes a psalm[62] in this connection can be an indication that his polemic is directed particularly against theologians and philosophers allied with theology.[63] The slumber of reason and the reveille of emotions is enough for them to consider themselves inspired and bring them to prophesize concerning state and morality. With a loose quotation from the speech which Fries had given at the festivities at the Wartburg on October 18, 1817, Hegel ridicules the former's praise of life, folk and friendship. From the discussion of piety which follows and from parallel passages such as the one in which Hegel alludes to Sand's murder of Kotzebue and De Wette's letter to Sand's mother (*Grl.* § 140A, pp. 143–144), however, we see that Hegel was aiming at a certain voguish form of theology *via* Fries, whom he had regarded as a philosophical lightweight even earlier. It is not impossible that he was even primarily thinking of his colleague Schleiermacher.[64]

Hegel's objection is not directed at feeling, life, folk and friendship as such. In many passages of his works he affirms and repeats that feeling is the first way in which we become aware of morality, right and religion, and "life" is one of his favorite images for indicating the concreteness and truth of reality. Hegel's target is the supposed self-satisfaction of immediate feeling and the unreflective appeal to "life" and other beautiful but naïve realities vulnerable to illusion and irrationality. The absolutizing of heart, soul and spirit closes one off from philosophy. For although philosophy begins with immediate experience (feeling, perception, and so on), it then goes on to a rigorous reconstruction by means of reason (and not under the directions of emotions and fantasies). Only reason is capable of discovering morality and the state as a self-contained, harmonious temple built according to necessary structures. Whoever sees it differently is blind to the architectonic in which the rationality at work in morality realizes itself. The temple of moral reason is collapsing before his eyes in the "sop" (Knox: "broth") of "heart, friendship and spirit". In the place of the institutions and proportions which should regulate public life he sees (and feels) only subjective and intersubjective sensitivities.

One thereby gives the state over to contingency, caprice and subjectivism. For feeling without reason is an opinion uncontrolled. If one rejects the necessary which only reason can reveal, all opinions and emotions are equally good and true. According to Epicurus the cosmos was ruled by chance. The quasi-philosophers (and theologians) of feeling raise contingency to the god and norm of the moral world. They do not realize that the ethical order of the state is a result that the intellect and reason have been working on for thousands of years[65] and they consider it a poor reality. The greatest danger however is to be found in their conviction that state and ethicity should also be ruled by opinion and caprice in the future, i.e., by subjective contingency. They save themselves the trouble of acquiring knowledge and insight, but thereby give themselves over – as did Faust – to the devil. For, the devil – or "evil" – consists, as *Grl.* § § 139–40 will explain, in the absolutizing of the viewpoint, interests and subjective choices of the individual subject who elevates himself to the decisive authority *against* the universality of reason.[66]

The contempt for science which is found in the philosophy (and theology) of feeling tries in various ways to obtain authority, e.g., by appealing to the Bible and posing as piety. Hegel makes a clear allusion here to Sand's motivations in the murder of Kotzebue and to De Wette's partial apology for Sand. The conflict between (supposed) piety and politics which is inherent to the disputed form of philosophy and theology found a dramatic expression in that murder. But state and piety do not have to come into conflict with one another. The condemnation of the political order in the name of religious feelings is a distortion of the true relation between religion and politics.

What Hegel says here about this relation is difficult to understand without an analysis of other passages in which he treats it more extensively, such as *Grl.* § 270 A, *Enc.* BC. 552 Remark and certain sections of the *Philosophy of Religion*. The issue is very important, also for an understanding of Hegel's fundamental motivation and vision, but an analysis of the *Preface* may be limited to the formulation of the optic contained in its text.[67]

When piety sets itself off against the laws of morality, it is a sign that that piety is irrational and false. For since religion and ethicity, if they are pure, both come forth from the same spirit and reason, they cannot come into conflict with one another. The proper relation between them consists in their both embodying the *same* truth in their own individual ways: the truth (or idea) which is developed in the ethical order as an "organic realm", i.e., as a totality of objective institutions (laws, powers, ethical customs), makes itself known in another way in piety: not as a public order, but as a concentrated, simple reality (God, who incarnates himself in the world and humanity in order to unite himself to them), a unity which the religious subject is aware of through intuition and feeling. Hegel thus thinks the relation between piety (or religion) and politics by means of their being identical with respect to *content* (they realize and know the same truth) and their being different in *form*: the element of ethicity is externality, unfolding publicness, objectivity; that of religious experience is inwardness, concentration, concealment, subjectivity. The objective laws of the state represent the day; piety's lack of differentiation is a domain of darkness or night. The criterion for the truth of "inner religion" lies in the objective truth of ethicity. According to Hegel, only the latter is "a truth in and for itself". That is why it is elevated above the subjective form of religious feeling.

The theologians of feeling turn this all around when they promote their pious feelings to the criterion for public laws. It is a pity that Hegel only polemizes here against false piety and does not explicitly state that politics and the state can also be false, and that in history they often are and to a certain extent have always been such. If he had more clearly discussed the possibility of a public and objective but untrue (and thus not "objective") order,[68] the problem of the relation between religion and politics would have been shown to be more complicated than the text in question suggests. As opposed to a true ethicity, then, we would find both a true form of religion and piety, which peacefully co-exists with ethicity, and a pseudo-religiosity, which conflicts with it. In opposition to pure religion, however, we find not only a pure ethicity but also a pseudo-ethicity, one which through its objective laws and powerful organization might suggest that it is genuine and good but which can very well be a form of institutionalized injustice. In his writings on Socrates and Jesus Hegel thematized such a situation.[69] It is not *a priori* impossible that such a situation is that of Germany or Europe in 1820, as Hegel's opponents think. Hegel's argument cannot consist in a reference to the objective and public character of the existing order, for these, as opposed to certain subjective feelings and intuitions, can have a bad content. He will first have to *prove* that the truth of *existing* ethicity is "in and for itself" – and in that sense "objective" – by comparing that which exists to the necessary structure and content demanded by the concept. The *Preface* thus presupposes the correctness of the justification given by the body of the *Philosophy of Right*.

It is true, not taking the content into consideration, that a philosophy or theology which rejects that objectivity and legality *as such* or replaced them with the feelings and opinions of just any subjects is thereby unsuited for a true illumination of ethicity. It is mistaken with reference to the essential nature and fundamental categories by which ethicity, as "objective spirit", is characterized. Whether Fries and the others criticized championed this form of subjectivism and sentimentalism would have to be historically researched. In opposition to Hegel they could well argue that they wanted *another* order and *differently* determined laws, based on true, as yet unrealized (and thus still inner and subjective) principles (e.g., "human rights"). And they could also accuse Hegel of having too subjective or even subjectivistic a conception of religion. Can one contend that religion is the second highest form of absolute spirit and also maintain that it is *merely* the *internal* moment of an order, the entire objectivity and publicness of which are found in ethicity, which Hegel – unjustly and in contradiction to his own principles[70] – identifies with the state?

Paragraph 9 (p. XIII–XIV)

The particular form of guilty conscience revealed by the type of eloquence in which such superficiality flaunts itself may be brought to your attention here and above all if you notice that when it is furthest from spirit, super-

> ficiality speaks most of spirit, when its talk is the most tedious dead-and-alive stuff, its favourite words are 'life' and 'vitalize', and when it gives evidence of the pure selfishness of baseless pride, the word most on its lips is 'people'. But the special mark which it carries on its brow is the hatred of law. Right and ethicity, and the actual world of right and the ethical (*des Sittlichen*), are understood through thoughts; through thoughts they are invested with a rational form, i.e. with universality and determinacy. This form is law; and this it is which the feeling that stipulates for its own whim, the conscience that places right in subjective convictions, has reason to regard as its chief foe. The form in which the right appears as a duty and a law it feels as the letter, cold and dead, as a shackle; for it does not recognize itself in the law and so does not recognize itself as free there, because law is the reason of the thing, and reason refuses to allow feeling to warm itself at its own particularity. Hence law, as I have remarked somewhere in the course of this text-book, is *par excellence* the shibboleth which marks out these false friends and comrades of what they call the 'people'.[71]

On the basis of his accusation that the philosophy of feeling is not only a criticism of the existing order but an aversion to universality, objectivity and legality as such, Hegel gives a psychological interpretation here of several typical characteristics which he observes in his opponents. Hegel diagnoses those characteristics, just as he does in the long Remark to section 140 concerning evil in the form of the guilty conscience, as symptoms of a half-conscious, half-unconscious hypocrisy. Considering the fact that all people essentially are and remain rational, even if they do deny reason in their chaotic behavior or false theories, every untruth presupposes a discrepancy between what is explicitly said or done and the hidden knowledge contained in the rational core of a human being. It can be called a hypocritical conscience, in so far as it takes credit for precisely those things it lacks – just as the hypocrite who claims to have virtues which he does not have. The verbosity with which the philosophy of feeling hides its ignorance exhausts itself in paraphrases of "people", "spirit" and "life"; these however in no way bear witness to a living spirit or a unity with what those philosophers call "the people". Anyone who knows that truth and spirit imply universality can hear how spiritless, dead and boring, how self-centered and how arrogant those paraphrases are.

The characteristic of a guilty conscience (even if it poses as a clear conscience) is hatred of the law. Under "law" in the explanation of this statement given in paragraph 9 is meant nothing other than the formal legality peculiar to all rational realities. "Law" here is synonymous with "thought" or "rational form". This form is explained with the help of the words "universality" and "determinacy" (*Bestimmtheit*) which must be understood as moments implying one another: rational universality is not an abstract notion, as the intellect would have it, but an individual reality. The determinate universal is the concrete concept, existing and understood as unity of universality, particularity and singularity.[72] The rational form is at the same time "the reason of the thing" (*die Vernunft der Sache*).

A philosophy that makes feeling the criterion of truth cannot recognize the (determinate) universality of the concept (or "thought" or "law") as the highest authority. It necessarily sees "the law" as its greatest enemy, because feeling, according to Hegel, is the element of individuality and not of universality, so that the absolutizing of feeling necessarily implies a rejection of the universal (and thus of the individuality integrated in a concept).

Just as is the case with every other rational reality, so, too, do right and state have a rational and in that sense universal structure. For the individual subject they assume the form of *duties* and *laws*. Whoever protests against positive law because and to the extent that right and state are formulated in the form of a universality ("law") thereby betrays his aversion to duty and right. His "conscientious" proclamations conceal and manifest his immorality. The young Hegel himself knew this aversion and translated it into precisely those words quoted here: besides "heart", "feeling", "life" and epiphets such as "beautiful", "sublime", "noble" and "great", Hegel's key terms for attacking the existing morality and moral philosophy were the "cold dead letter" [of the law] and especially the "chains" or "shackles" (*Fesseln*) borrowed from Rousseau.[73] Fortunately for him the "sins of his youth" were not yet published when he later found and criticized them in the speeches and books of his contemporaries.[74] In the meantime he discovered that an appeal to subjective feelings and conceptions which does not allow for integration into objective and universal structures is an expression of a kind of narcissism: it is no longer the *issue* that is at stake but a mistaken subjectivity. By cutting himself off from the universal, an individual gives in to the temptation to withdraw into his own intimate world. The price of the warmth of this nest is his true self-possession and freedom, for these consist in the realization of his rationality, i.e., his concrete universality. The basic mistake of the subjectivistic philosophy is its lack of understanding of the true meaning of "self". That is why it cannot recognize its true self and freedom in the laws of the state.[75]

Once again we see that Hegel's argumentation is indecisive with regard to the question of whether the existing laws, duties and rights are good and rational. It is concerned only with the *idea* of right, ethicity, duty and conscience. One can accept his entire argument and yet precisely on the basis of this argument state that the Prussia of 1820 did *not* satisfy the true notion and the true laws of right, state and ethicity, for example due to the fact that there were too many irrational power structures and too much caprice in that system. Through the ambiguity of the word "law", Hegel's argument can impress a superficial reader as a condemnation of those in favor of a correction or reform of the state. Perhaps – for example considering censorship – he consciously made use of this ambiguity. But it cannot have been his intention to identify the idea of law with the actual order. Not only does he clearly distinguish these in *Grl.* § 3+A, but through its incongruence with the existing conditions, the unfolding of the concept of right in the *Philosophy of Right* also implies a criticism of the concrete content of the actual order in the name of the true concept of the only partially realized ideal ethicity.

Paragraph 10 (p. XIV–XVI)

> At the present time, the pettifoggery of caprice (*Willkür*) has usurped the name of philosophy and succeeded in giving a wide public the opinion that such triflings are philosophy. The result of this is that it has now become almost a disgrace to go on speaking in philosophical terms about the nature of the state, and law-abiding men cannot be blamed if they become impatient so soon as they hear mention of a philosophical science of the state. Still less is it a matter for surprise that governments have at last directed their attention to this kind of philosophy, since, apart from anything else, philosophy with us is not, as it was with the Greeks for instance, pursued as a private skill, but has an existence in the open, in contact with the public, and especially, or even only, in the service of the state. Governments have proved their trust in their scholars who have made philosophy their chosen field by leaving entirely to them the construction and contents of philosophy – though here and there, if you like, it may not have been so much confidence that has been shown as indifference to science itself, and professorial chairs of philosophy have been retained only as a tradition (in

France, for instance, to the the best of my knowledge, chairs of metaphysics at least have been allowed to lapse). Their confidence, however, has very often been ill repaid, or alternatively, if you preferred to see indifference, you would have to regard the result, the decay of thorough knowledge, as the penalty of this indifference. Prima facie, superficiality seems to be extremely accommodating, one might say, at least in relation to public peace and order, because it fails to touch or even to guess at the substance of the things; no action, or at least no police action, would thus have been taken against it in the first instance, had it not been that there still existed in the state a need for a deeper education and insight, a need which the state required philosophical science to satisfy. On the other hand, superficial thinking about the ethical, about right and duty in general, leads automatically to the maxims which constitute superficiality in this sphere, i.e. to the principles of the Sophists which are so clearly outlined for our information in Plato. What is right these principles locate in subjective aims and opinions, in subjective feeling and particular conviction, and from them there follows the ruin of the inner ethicity and a good conscience, of love and right dealing between private persons, no less than the ruin of public order and the law of the land. The significance which such phenomena must acquire for governments cannot be denied by the pretentiousness which has used that very grant of confidence and the authority of a professorial chair to support the demand that the state should uphold and give scope to what corrupts the substantial source of achievement, namely universal principles, and so even to the defiance of the state as if such defiance were all right. 'If God gives a man an office, he also gives him brains' is an old joke which in these days surely no one will take wholly in earnest.[76]

The preceding discussion contrasted a "superficial" (*seicht*) philosophy to the method of true philosophy. Paragraphs 10 and 11 replace the opposition of a true and false philosophy of right with another opposition: they treat the relation between politics and philosophy and the reactions of the state to bad types of philosophy.

The idea that the distortion of right implied by an illegitimate philosophy has brought all of philosophy into discredit was already expressed in paragraph 7. It is repeated with the help of the word "disgrace". A second result of that distorted right is "the impatience" with which law-abiding (*rechtlich*) people react (not being able to stand the situation and calling for repressive measures). The third reaction, that of the state itself by means of its government, is not only the most dramatic one (it was expressed in 1820 for example by strict censorship and the dismissal of several professors), but within the framework of a philosophy of right and state also the most essential. The following two paragraphs are concerned with this. They do not mention specific measures, but they do express a justification in principle, in light of government measures already taken, of correct action by the state with regard to instruction and publications in the field of philosophy.

The point of departure for this justification is that philosophy in the contemporary state is not a private but a public activity. In Greece philosophy could still be limited to an elite or a school, but in our times it reaches a much larger public. The reason for this difference is not given. We are in all probability to think of both the extension of literacy and education (*Bildung*) and the character of the *Zeitgeist*, which synthesizes the subjectivity of each individual with the greatest possible universality and makes itself known as much in philosophy as on the political level. Philosophy's public character finds expression in the fact that most philosophers are no longer private thinkers or teachers, as were Socrates and Plotinus, but state officials. Those who are not public servants have a more than local influence through their publications, but Hegel speaks further only about those who practice philosophy in service of the state.[77]

If Hegel's point of departure is correct, it is obvious that the state must watch over the proper performance of the function of philosopher. But even aside from this it is clear that the state must protect itself from activities that undermine it. If certain philosophies endanger the state's foundation and morals, the state must necessarily respond with repressive measures. The same is true of religion: if certain words and ideas have enough power to uproot the ethical order, then the ethical order must fight back, *and if the existing order is a rational one*, it is correct in doing so.[78]

The necessary addition of the final "if" is passed over silently by Hegel because he obviously believes that the existing order and the measures taken are at least for the most part justified. The text even suggests that the state should have been on the lookout sooner. For, indeed, the current irrationality in the field of political philosophy is a result of the carelessness of which the government is guilty. This carelessness can be interpreted in two ways, one more and one less generous: the result is the same.

The fact that the government has hitherto involved itself so little which philosophy and philosophers can be attributed to the great confidence which it had in scholars. Through the development of philosophy, however, it has become apparent that this trust was too trusting: the social critics have repaid it poorly. One can also be of the opinion that the government set *too little* store in philosophy. Because it thought philosophy useless or impractical, it was totally indifferent to professorial theorizing. But that has been its downfall: because it had no watchful eye cast on philosophy, it must now pay the penalty (*ein Büszen dieser Gleichgültigkeit*).

To the state's taking action against philosophy – and to the actual action of the state, which Hegel not only tries to understand here but also, at least implicitly, supports – one could object that such action is unnecessary if the philosophy in question is superficial, does not get to the heart of the matter, and thus cannot do much harm. The tolerant political view represented by this objection has Hegel's sympathy: in the long Remark to section 319 on freedom of the press he comes out in favor of a "tolerance" (*eine Duldung*) which consists in contempt.[79] But this cannot be the entire answer to the question of a proper reaction. On the positive side, the state must also assure the satisfaction of the need for a solid education and for those insights which can only be expected from true science. For this reason it must not only despise the naïveté of the denounced philosophers, it must also fight it. If the state is the greatest educator – and Hegel accepts this Platonic point of departure – then it must use its power to crush ideologies threatening its existence. Hegel sees himself as a Plato fighting against the Sophists (but Socrates is notably absent!).[80] Those who adulate subjective feelings, ends and opinions (δόξαι) weaken the true principles and foundations of right and ethicity and have a destructive influence in the intersubjective order as well as in public institutions. When subjective choice or *Willkür* reigns supreme, morality, love and right are impossible. The government, which is primarily concerned with ensuring the existence and the principles of a just society, has the right and the duty to take over. Against this right and duty one cannot appeal to one's supposed rights as public servant and professor, for these rights are based precisely on the trust bestowed by the state, which has been betrayed.

Hegel presupposes here that the state and the state alone can determine which theories of state, morality and right are destructive. A philosophy professor has no recourse if the state withdraws its trust in him. A juridical power which could settle a dispute between state (king and government) and public servant is unthinkable in Hegel's view, for an authority higher than the state is a contradiction in terms.

Paragraph 11 (p. XVI–XVIII)

In the fresh importance which circumstances have led governments to attach to the character of philosophical work, there is one element which we cannot fail to notice; this is the protection and support which the study of philosophy now seems to have come to need in several other directions. Think of the numerous publications in the field of the positive sciences, as well as edifying religious works and vague literature of other kinds, which reveal to their readers the contempt for philosophy I have already mentioned, in that, although the thought in them is immature to the last degree and philosophy is entirely alien to them, they treat it as something over and done with. More than this, they expressly rail against it and pronounce its content, namely the conceptual (*begreifende*) knowledge of God, the natural and spiritual world, the knowledge of truth, to be a foolish and even sinful presumptuousness, while reason, and again reason, and reason repeated *ad infinitum* is arraigned, disparaged, and condemned. At the very least such writings reveal to us that, to a majority of those engaged in activities supposedly scientific, the claims of the concept are an embarrassment which none the less they cannot escape. I venture to say that anyone with such phenomena before him may very well begin to think that, if they alone are considered, tradition is now neither worthy of respect nor sufficient to secure for the study of philosophy either tolerance or existence as a public institution.* The arrogant declamations current in our time against philosophy present the singular spectacle, on the one hand of deriving their justification from the superficiality to which that study has been degraded, and, on the other, of being themselves rooted in this element against which they turn so ungratefully. For by pronouncing the knowledge of truth a wild-goose chase, this self-styled philosophizing has reduced all thoughts and all topics to the same level, just as the despotism of the Roman Empire abolished the distinction

* I came across a similar view in a letter of Joh. von Müller (*Werke*, Part vii, p. 56). In talking of the state of Rome in 1803 when the city was under French control, he says: 'Asked how the public educational institutions were faring, a professor replied *On les tolère comme les bordels*.' The so-called 'Doctrine of Reason', logic namely, we can indeed still hear recommended, perhaps with the conviction that it is such a dry and profitless science that nobody will busy himself with it, or that of here and there a man does take it up, he will thereby acquire mere empty formulae, unproductive and innocuous, and that therefore in either case the recommendation will do no harm, even if it does no good.

> between free men and slaves, virtue and vice, honour and dishonour, learning and ignorance. The result of this levelling process is that the concepts of what is true, the laws of the ethical, likewise become nothing more that opinions and subjective convictions. The maxims of the worst of criminals, since they too are convictions, are put on the same level of value as those laws; and at the same time any object, however sorry, however accidental, any material however insipid, is put on the same level of value as what constitutes the interest of all thinking men and the bonds of the ethical world.[81]

In paragraph 10 Hegel had argued that the government of the various states (he is thinking of Austria and the various German territories) were correct in taking measures against certain kinds of (political) philosophy. In the eleventh paragraph he states that the governments also have a positive role with respect to philosophy: when it is endangered by poor philosophers or blasphemers, the state must provide its support and protection.

A large number of scientific publications, tracts and other literature,[82] the nature of which is unclear, not only express the contempt for philosophy discussed in paragraph 7 but explicitly take up arms against it. By denying that the truth can be known about God, nature and spirit and by considering reason to be the great evildoer, both philosophy's true content and method as well as its right to exist are undermined. Hegel is thinking here of empirical scientists, but also and especially of theologians who consider the philosophical claim that reason can understand nature, spirit and even God to be a "sinful pretension". Anti-philosophy is fashionable. Strengthened by the discredit into which the sophists of feeling have brought all philosophy, it has led to a practically total ban of philosophy from public life.[83] An old and respectable tradition has it that philosophers must have a place in the state, and that their work must at least be met with tolerance. The joint influence of pesudo-philosophers and anti-philosophers has destroyed the power of this tradition. Against the machinations of anti-philosophy, philosophy needs the support of a power other than that of tradition: the *political* power of the government, which must protect philosophy as an essential element of cultural life. University professors have a special right to protection above and beyond this, because they are government appointees.

Hegel's appeal to the power of the government may cause some surprise. Is true philosophy (Reason's noblest product!) not itself strong enough to convince its opponents? To what extent is it impossible for it to exist without the protection of an extra-philosophical power? Will such a protection not extend itself to decisions about the kind of programs, the chairs, the appointments and publications in the field of philosophy that are to be deemed acceptable? Is philosophy not abandoned to the state and its insights by such an appeal for protection? And what if that insight is not justified? Hegel will say that it is precisely those professors of philosophy appointed by the state who must guarantee that the state is guided by true insight. But how can a philosopher prevent the powerful's being inspired by pseudo-philosophers or anti-philosophers?

Hegel offers a noble motive here for the legitimation which he, as a good public servant, gives: the defense of true philosophy against both the sophistry of pseudo-philosophers who undermine right, state and morals and the anti-philosophers who want to destroy it altogether. We see that Hegel considered himself to be in the right in these matters by a letter discussed by Rosenkranz which was written to Altenstein, the minister of education, between February and July 1822.[84] After a critical review of the *Philosophy of Right* had appeared which ended with the accusation that Hegel's stand against Fries "seems like the mocking and deliberately insulting of an already broken man",[85] Hegel wrote to Altenstein that he – according to Rosenkranz – "desired protection by the Department of Education from this denunciation". He found it intolerable that a Prussian public servant could be made suspect in a publication printed in Prussia with Prussian subsidies. He had not at all thought of Fries as a private individual, only of his pernicious theses. "By his criticism of a person who thought himself to be privileged and who was accustomed to having the final word in things, he wanted to give the department an example of what a liberal freedom of the press could lead to"![86]

After discussing the relationship between political power and false forms, Hegel concludes his accusation of pseudo-philosophy in the second half of paragraph 11 by presenting it as a breeding ground for the tirades against philosophy which are in fashion. But in doing so he also refutes anti-philosophy itself, which probably had supporters in government circles, too, and comes out in favor of tolerance and protection for true philosophy. The argumentation runs as follows.

The fact that some people today are reacting so strongly and so vociferously to philosophy (on the basis of the discredit into which pseudo-philosophy has brought all philosophers, even true ones) is itself an expression of pseudo-philosophy. (Certain governmental authorities are thus being criticized here to the extent that they take action against philosophy: they are themselves exponents of pseudo-philosophy and fight unjustly against *every* form of philosophy). For while that pseudo-philosophy which calls itself philosophy proclaims its liberality – we would say its "democratic" character – it is in fact the worst sort of despotism. The modern sophist is a leveller of all thoughts and ideas, just as were the Roman emperors, according to Hegel's interpretation in his *Philosophy of World History* and elsewhere.[87] Everyone is just as correct as the next person: qualitative differences no longer exist. The true notions and laws of right, morality and politics are worth just as much as convictions and theses diametrically opposed to them. Criminality is just as good as civil obedience. The foundations of ethicity from which people derive their freedom and dignity are not distinguished from insignificant details and whims.[88] True philosophy and its insights are thus degraded to the level of an unimportant and indifferent opinion. In this way the "liberalism" of the "critical philosophers" reveals itself as a tiranny[89] more repressive than that of the politicians it accuses.

Those who distrust and contest *all* philosophy, like the positive scientists and theologians mentioned above, legitimate themselves by pointing out the destructive character of pseudo-philosophy, which they cannot distinguish from true philosophy. But their own arguments are derived from the very pseudo-philosophy they deny. For they, too, think that philosophy is nothing but the spouting of opinions on any subject. If they knew what reason's actual demands and methods were, they would know what genuine philosophy is; they would then no longer distrust philosophy but would attack sophistry in the name of true philosophy alone.

The preliminary conclusion Hegel gives here summarizes the first part of the *Preface* (par. 2–11): Hegel's critique of a certain kind of *pseudo-philosophy* has made clear that it could lead (unjustly) to a massive *anti-philosophy*. But anti-philosophy is itself a kind of pseudo-philosophy which it incorrectly confuses with *true philosophy*. The latter is the only proper criterion for judging and organizing the relations between politics and philosophy in its three forms of genuine, pseudo- and anti-philosophy. The statement that those in power should allow as their advisors only true philosophers and not sophists (even if they are theologians!) or enemies of philosophy is not made explicitly here, but for a good reader that message is clearly contained in the text.

Paragraph 12 (p. XVIII–XIX)

> It is therefore to be taken as a piece of *luck* for philosophic science – though in actual fact, as I have said, it is the *necessity* of the thing – that this philosophizing which like an exercise in scholasticism might have continued to spin its web in seclusion, has now been put into closer touch and so into open variance with actuality, in which the principles of rights and duties are serious matter, and which lives in the light of its consciousness of these. It is just this placing of philosophy in the actual world which meets with misunderstandings, and so I revert to what I have said before, namely that, since philosophy is the exploration of the rational, it is for that very reason the apprehension of the present and the actual, not the erection of a beyond, supposed to exist, God knows where, or rather which exists, and we can perfectly well say where, namely in the error of a one-sided, empty, ratiocination. In the course of this book, I have remarked that even Plato's *Republic*, which passes proverbially as an empty ideal, is in essence nothing but an interpretation of the nature of Greek ethical life. Plato was conscious that there was breaking into that life in his own time a deeper principle which could appear in it directly only as a longing still unsatisfied, and so only as something corruptive. To combat it, he needs must have sought aid from that very longing itself. But this aid had to come from on High and all that Plato could do was to seek it in the first place in a particular external form of that same Greek ethical life. By that means he thought to master this corruptive invader, and thereby he did fatal injury to the deeper impulse which underlay it, namely free infinite personality. Still, his genius is proved by the fact that the principle on which the distinctive character of his Idea of the state turns is precisely the pivot on which the impending world revolution turned at that time.[90]

This paragraph begins the second part of the *Preface*. Although the polemical tone is maintained, Hegel now concentrates on a more positive treatment of the relations between philosophy and ethical reality than was given before. The transition from the first to the second part is made by an interpretation of the conflict that has broken out between the existing ethical reality and the superficial "philosophy" shown to be unphilosophical. The rupture with the state, proclaimed by this philosophy through its criticism and effectuated by the measures taken by the state, manifests the contradiction between a shallow theory held in the closed milieu of the universities, as a game without consequences, and the living reality in which the rights, duties and foundations of ethicity are taken seriously.[91] True theory however is also serious. It can therefore not come into conflict with true ethiciy (only with untrue, non-serious or corrupt forms of right and politics, mentioned below by Hegel only implicitly or indirectly.) The conflict between pseudo-philosophy and the state is a fortunate one for science, for it unmasks the immorality of pseudo-philosophy and frees true science of that caricature. Through the public rupture the real problem and the root of all discussions, misunderstandings and tensions has come to light: it is the question of *the relation of philosophy to reality*.

Pickung up again on paragraph 7, Hegel formulates his ideas concerning this relation in a thesis which the rest of the *Preface* paraphrases and explains.

As the examination and understanding of the rational, philosophy is not the invention of a Utopia or hereafter but the comprehension of the reality of here and now. A Utopia is nothing other than a mental image. Its unreality is proof of the fact that it is not true, for truth consists not in abstract thoughts – they are only one moment of truth – but in a solid, empirical reality insofar as it realizes adequate thoughts. Utopian fantasies are absolutized abstractions without power; their defenders are unrealistic fanatics who cannot handle reality.

In his rejection of ideas that do not correspond to the actual situation, Hegel does not differentiate between Utopian or unrealizable models and ideas of a future situation unrealizable now but possible at a later stage. He cannot absolutely reject the latter, because then every attempt to improve an existing situation would be impossible. The *Philosophy of Right* contains many suggestions for improving the existing legal order,[92] and the historical developments which resulted in the contemporary situation were at least partly caused by thinkers and men of action who formed an image of the future and then realized it either completely or to a degree. Not every discrepancy between the conceived and the existing reality is irrational. Thinking is not just the copying of the facts as they happen to be but the discovering of universal and necessary structures and of the reasons why reality must be the way it is. But actuality contains more than a universal and necessary, comprehensible and rational structure: besides contingencies, which cannot be deduced, it also exhibits distortions, perversions and incorrect renditions of the true reality revealed by thought. Hegel points out in a later defense of the *Preface* that not everything that exists is also "actual" in the strictest sense of the term, which includes rationality (i.e., necessity and a solid grounding).[93] With this statement Hegel himself admits that even a genuine philosopher is incapable of justifying all that exists. Philosophy even understands that evil is an essential element of the existing reality.[94] Thus he must be aware of the fact that the actual condition of the world, state, right and history will be partly incorrect and bad. Criticism of the currently functioning legal system and actual politics is therefore a self-evident part of a philosophy which tries to understand and explain the (relative) rationality of the juridical and political reality. Hegel's polemic therefore cannot be directed against all forms of criticism, but only against a fundamental refusal to recognize that the existing order is at least partially rational, and against a kind of thinking which believes that rationality exists only or primarily in abstract thoughts and not in the living reality of history.

Even a Utopia or a seemingly "empty ideal" is not necessarily viewed by Hegel as an indication of immorality or stupidity. It *can* be the expression of a great and near-real thought, the whole truth of which is hindered by the situation of the times. The polemic against Fries and others like him is given extra relief by Hegel's contrasting their thought to another, truly philosophical Utopia. If Fries could be compared to Plato, his protest would have a totally different meaning than it now has. Is Hegel suggesting in the passage on Plato to be discussed here that a certain kind of criticism of the existing order of right and state *is* justified?

The image of the *res publica* or society which Plato creates in the *Republic* (and which he futilely tried to realize in Sicily) is the proverbial example of an "empty idea". "Platonic" is synonymous with unreal, not actual. It therefore seems to fall under Hegel's criticism of abstractions. And yet Plato is a political philosopher of the highest order. Not only does Hegel recognize this: a careful analysis of the *Philosophy of Right* makes clear that it includes many of Plato's ideas on state and justice, and that they play even a greater role than those of the "realist" Aristotle.[95] The greatness of the *Republic* consists in its providing the insight of Plato, a true philosopher, into the existing reality of his place, culture and time. But this reality was involved in a crisis: the ancient *polis* had outlived its greatness and had declined under the influence of a new, un-Greek principle which had surreptitiously undermined it. An adequate concept of the actuality had to show both moments of this situation: the peculiar nature of Greek ethicity and the beginnings of its destruction due to the intrusive new principle.

The new principle Hegel speaks of here and in many other places is the "principle of subjectivity", which together with the principle of universality makes up the ground pattern of Hegel's philosophy of right. According to this view this principle came into the world with Christianity, although Socrates had had an intuition of it.[96] This principle declares the right of the individual human subject to will, to act, to be and to be recognized as an individual by society and other human beings.[97] This right was not known in antiquity (unless in the prophetic consciousness of Socrates). In section 185 A of the *Philosophy of Right*, to which the present passage of the *Preface* refers, it is stated as follows: "The principle of the *independent, in itself infinite personality* of the individual, the principle of subjective freedom which arose, as inner principle, in the *Christian* religion and externally and thus in connection with abstract universality – in the *Roman* world, is not done justice in the Greek, merely substantial form of actual spirit". It is on the basis of this principle, the discovery of the individual, that the modern world differs from the Greek polis, which could make no room for the independence of the "free infinite personality" but rather saw and treated individual citizens *only* as parts of the whole.

Due to the fact that Greek ethicity was not able to integrate the particularity of individual subjects, Hegel calls it a "substantial ethicity" (*Grl.* § 185 A). The philosophical elucidation which Plato gives of it is a concept of the state as substance. The principle of subjectivity is a "*deeper* principle" in so far as a substance which is not also a subject is not yet an adequate realization of spirit. It is only when spirit realizes itself in the form of autonomous willing, i.e., of freedom which knows and wills itself, that a truly human society is possible. But to this end it is necessary for the *individual* will to come into its own and be recognized, for *outside* the wills of individuals freedom has no existence or presence. To exist as a universal *will*, i.e., as free self-affirmation, the universal (ethical substance) must realize itself in and as the willing and acting here and now of individual subjects.

For Plato, totally rooted in the Greek *polis*, this insight inspired by Rousseau and Kant could not yet be clear. His political philosophy is an analysis of substantial ethicity in all its splendor. But he distinguishes himself from most other thinkers – and herein consists his greatness – by anticipating the principle which was then developing and making it a central theme of his political philosophy. As may be expected of a great philosopher, he thematized the new principle in a way which corresponded to the peculiar nature of the situation. Socrates had awakened the consciousness of the individual subject's absoluteness, but the actual situation of *polis*, right and morals did not allow a realization of individual rights. The consciousness of this right thus necessarily remained unsatisfied, so that it took on the form of an unfulfilled desire, the fulfilment of which was, at least for the time being, impossible. As an unsatisfied desire seeking possibilities for satisfaction, however, this new consciousness – the call for recognition of the individual as a subject having inviolable rights – was at the same time a corrupting influence within Greek ethicity. The form in which the principle of subjectivity appeared in Plato's time could be none other than that of a "longing", which brought about the collapse of the existing order and thus had to be considered decadent. As a philosopher of the here and now, Plato had to thematize this decadence and integrate the new principle (which was in opposition to the existing order but which he observed both within and outside himself) into his synthesis of the ethical order. As a true Greek, he could do nothing but hold tight to the established order of the harmonious *polis* and counter the new principle as a danger. In order to save the *res publica* at a time when the desire for the subjects' independence and the privatization of welfare and well-being were beginning to make themselves known, he suggested abolishing private property and the family and rejected the freedom of choice of profession.[98] Plato's communism, which was to suppress the individual subjects' tendencies to find themselves more important than the universal, was a "special form" of the ethical order which he sketched. Since he experienced the principle of subjectivity as an irresistable tendency but could not integrate it into the *polis*, he took refuge in a violent repression. The true solution of the opposition, which Plato could not manage, the true "assistance" against the danger of privatization, had to come from "on high", out of "the heavens": it is only through Christ, the incarnation of God in an individual human subject, that the two fundamental principles of society (the general and the individual) are reconciled. Plato "fatally injured" the deeper principle" and "deeper impulse", but he was still a great philosopher because his philosophy captured the actual world of his time (together with its inner contradictions and impossibilities) in corresponding ideas. The self-evident harmony of the old *polis* was a thing of the past, and a new desire made itself known but *could* not yet realize itself in a rational way. Plato's Utopia (with violence!) was the expression of an "impossible" reality.[99]

Socrates did recognize the positive meaning of the principle of subjectivity, but he, too, landed in an insoluble contradiction by doing so. As opposed to the philosopher, who understands (ethical) reality *after* it is realized and is at the point of going into decline (as Hegel says in paragraph 19), Socrates rather is a prophet who sees the quintessence of the future but cannot show how this is to be translated into reality. With his forward-looking vision Socrates was indeed the great corruptor of the *polis* and its youth, who under his influence no longer wanted to accept the old order. In this way Socrates, just as Antigone, was guilty. His prophesying was an undermining of the only reality which universality in his time could have: that of the existing, albeit fading, Greek rationality.[100]

What can we learn about Hegel's philosophy of right from his very concentrated interpretation of Plato's significance for a philosophy of right and politics? It is clear – and the following paragraphs strengthen this idea – that Plato accomplished the task of the philosopher in an exemplary fashion, notwithstanding his historically conditioned inability to solve the most essential contradiction constituting the ethical problematic. Hegel *is* able to resolve the tension between the two fundamental principles of politics. The long history of Christianity *via* the Roman Empire, the Middle Ages, the Reformation and the French Revolution has developed ethical reality to the point that it is now possible to conceptually reconstruct it in a way which does justice to both principles: the modern state – just as the Concept – is a unity of the universal and the individual by means of the particular. The recognition of the right of subjectivity which Socrates demanded from the ancient *polis* can now be understood as an organic moment of the ethical order. There is therefore no longer any reason for protests like those of Fries and the like, who give themselves the airs of the prophet.

But does Hegel think it possible that his own time makes it impossible for him – as it was for Plato – to speak the perfect and final truth? Is he already suggesting here, and perhaps even more clearly in paragraph 19, that his own philosophy of right is also a looking back to an order already worn out, and that there are therefore reasons for nostalgia and prophetic vision which can prove to be true and actual? What Fries offers is in Hegel's view worthless. But could it be a symptom of a deeper dissatisfaction, one which could perhaps reveal itself in a more adequate way? Hegel sometimes compares his time to that of Socrates, and to the decline of the ancient world at the time of the Stoics.[101] But a concrete reference to a new ethical principle is difficult to find in his work. He seems rather to expect a further realization in the future of the foundations formulated in his philosophy of right. To this extent we can say that Hegel – just as Plato – had sympathy for those openly vindicating the rights of subjectivity. We can even find a veiled criticism of the Karlsbad resolutions in his criticism of Plato's violent repression of individual self-interest. These kinds of external measures do not resolve any fundamental tensions. A good state reconciles the contradictions by the way in which it is constituted and lives. Repression is just as bad a sign as rebellion. Both manifest a deficiency of synthesis.[102]

Paragraph 13 (p. XIX–XXI)

What is rational is actual
and what is actual is rational.[103]

On this conviction the plain man like the philosopher takes his stand, and from it philosophy starts in its study of the universe of spirit as well as the universe of nature. If reflection, feeling, or whatever form subjective consciousness may take, looks upon the present (*die Gegenwart*) as something vacuous (*ein Eitles*) and looks beyond it with the eyes of superior wisdom, it finds itself in a vacuum (*im Eiteln*), and because it is actual only in the present, it is itself mere vacuity (*Eitelkeit*). If on the other hand the Idea passes for 'only an idea', for something represented in an opinion, philosophy rejects such a view and shows that nothing is actual except the Idea. Once that is granted, the great thing is to apprehend in the show (*Schein*) of the temporal and transient the substance which is immanent and the eternal which is present. For since rationality (which is synonymous with the Idea) enters upon external existence simultaneously with its actualization, it emerges with an infinite wealth of forms, appearances and shapes, (*Formen,*

Erscheinungen und Gestaltungen). Around its heart (*Kern*) it throws a motley covering (*der bunten Rinde*) with which consciousness is at home to begin with, a covering which the concept has first to penetrate before it can find the inward pulse and feel it still beating in the outward appearances (*Gestaltungen*). But the infinite variety of circumstance which is developed in this externality by the light of the essence glinting in it (*durch das Scheinen des Wesens in sie*) – this endless material and its organization – this is not the subject matter of philosophy. To touch this at all would be to meddle with things to which philosophy is unsuited; on such topics it may save itself the trouble of giving good advice. Plato might have omitted (*konnte es unterlassen*) his recommendation to nurses to keep on the move with infants and to rock them continually in their arms. And Fichte too need not have carried what has been called the 'construction' of his passport regulations to such a pitch of perfection as to require suspects not merely to sign their passports but to have their likenesses painted on them. Along such tracks all trace of philosophy is lost, and such super-erudition it can the more readily disclaim since its attitude to this infinite multitude of topics should of course be most liberal. In adopting this attitude, philosophic science shows itself to be poles apart from the hatred with which the folly (*die Eitelkeit*) of superior wisdom regards a vast number of affairs and institutions, a hatred in which pettiness takes the greatest delight because only by venting it does it attain a feeling of its self-hood (*Selbstgefühl*).[104]

After indicating in paragraph 12 what the proper philosophical attitude is concerning reality, and after illustrating it using the example of Plato's political philosophy, which seems to express a different position, Hegel formulates the foundation of that attitude in a kind of dictum:

What is rational is actual,
and what is actual is rational.

In the following paragraphs, too, we find these kinds of proverbial formulations, around which Hegel groups his methodological considerations. Paragraphs 15–17, for example, have a sentence from Aesop as their starting point, which they combine with a reference to the Rosicrucians; paragraph 19 paraphrases Goethe's saying "All theory is gray". It also seems as if the motto of paragraph 13 is borrowed from someone else, or from one of Hegel's earlier works, but in spite of the strong resemblance to phrases of Parmenides and Aristotle and the conceptual agreement with the scholastic adages "Esse est intelligible" and "Ens et verum (intelligible) convertuntur" (the converse of which is clearly expressed in the motto) Hegel does not appear to be quoting himself or anyone else here. His verse-like and pseudo-poetic axiom functions like a riddle which must sharpen the reader's attention for the explanation now to follow.

That this explanation was insufficient has been made clear by the unending discussions which the riddle still invites. As early as 1827, with the second edition of the *Encyclopedia*, Hegel felt the need to correct a misunderstanding to which part of the *Preface* in particular had given rise. In the Remark to section 6 of the *Encyclopedia* Hegel states with a certain indignation that the word "actuality" (*Wirklichkeit*) which he had used was falsely taken to refer to the factual existence of what is. It seems clear that he contributed to this reading by introducing the term "actuality" as synonymous with " the present" (*das Gegenwärtige*) and contrasting it to the "other-worldliness" (*das Jenseitige*) of an empty, "Platonic" ideal (par. 12). But according to Hegel the text of paragraph 13 must be read in accordance with the distinctions he makes in the *Logic*, the *Encyclopedia* and the *Philosophy of Right* itself, distinctions which are given unclearly and incompletely in the present *Preface.*[105] At any rate a previous analysis of *Enc.* BC.6 + Remark and of *Grl.* § 1 + Remark is a good and almost imperative preparation for a good understanding of the *Preface.*

The sixth section of the Berlin version of the *Encyclopedia*[106] is part of an introductory consideration of the form and content of philosophy. Its object or content is identified here with the *world*, i.e., with that which consciousness finds within and outside of itself insofar as this can be understood as a content "which brings itself forth and is brought forth originally in the realm of living spirit." The last clause summarizes the structure and life of the Idea, the concept of which can only be achieved as a result of the entire *Logic.* But this much is already clear: actuality does not include everything which just happens to exist. Primary *experience*, in which all kinds of things appear, demands a consideration which distinguishes between the merely ephemeral and meaningless on the one hand, and the important or meaningful which remains the same and is eternal on the other. Hegel calls the former *appearance* (*Erscheinung*), in which he not only includes the contingent, but also all forms of evil, such as "error" and "every decadent existence".[107] *Actuality* (*Wirklichkeit*) is only that reality which is as good as it should be, the necessity of which can be understood by a thoroughgoing reason and which is thus necessarily good. Philosophy is the searching out and understanding of this "true reality", the recognition of the Idea which realizes itself in the external and internal worlds of consciousness. Philosophy is thus also a pointing out of those phenomena which are not the organic expression of the true core of reality but only contingent or mistaken "existence". As an insight into reality, philosophy corresponds with other ways of knowing true reality, such as those found in art and especially in religion. A *good*, i.e., *true* experience of the world has the same content as does philosophy. In that sense (true) experience is a touchstone to determine whether a philosophy is true or not, by comparing the content of experience to that of philosophy (although immediate experience can make no direct judgment about the form, i.e., the peculiar method, of philosophy). The highest goal of philosophy is to understand the rational, i.e., necessary, structure and content of the actuality we experience – a rationality which really exists in that actuality. The agreement between thinking and being which then arises unites the philosopher's consciousness with existing reality and reconciles the two, in spite of the meaningless and bad phenomena which are also involved in reality as fleeting deformations. But the correspondence between philosophy and naïve experience can only be "a(n external) touchstone" if it is *first* certain that that experience is genuine, and not, for example, an improper appreciation of superficial or mistaken realities, which are not "real" or "actual" although they do exist. But this in turn presupposes that there is a criterion for the truth of experiences *outside* philosophy. For example good taste, a feeling for pure piety or a solid intuition of true morality.

The reconciliation with reality can only be a characteristic of true philosophy if there is certainty beforehand concerning what not only *exists* in the factual order of things (e.g., in the order of state and right), but must also be called *actual* "in an emphatic sense", i.e., if the philosopher can base his thought on a non-philosophical but *true* knowledge or experience concerning reality, one which has *already* made a distinction between truth (actuality) and mere appearance. With reference to the state this means that the external criterion *rests on* a previous, non-philosophical certainty, one which separates the good from the bad elements of the established order. True philosophy thus presupposes a non-philosophical but true knowledge – a sort of conscience – of reality, one which philosophy merely needs to understand.

The distinctions we are making here are ignored by Hegel in *Enc.* § 6. The way in which he speaks of an external testing of philosophy by reference to experience and of its reconciliation with reality as a reconciliation of true thinking and "*existing* rationality" can lead one to believe that he identifies the factual situation, at least for the most part, with true reality. To avoid this misunderstanding, he should have at least pointed out that the "external touchstone" which is found in the correspondence of thought and reality is not simply there for the taking but is itself the result of a purification transforming the initial experience of the factual situation into a *pure experience* of reality, one which at the same time realizes the extent to which actuality is transformed by unreal, contingent and bad facts. One can suspect that Hegel is using the ambiguity of the word *Wirklichkeit* (which can also be taken in the sense of factual reality) in this passage, too. If actuality is distinguished from appearance only by its inner necessity and not by the fact that it exists, then it is identical to "*rational*" reality, and the statement that "everything which is "actual" (*wirklich*) is also "rational" is an analytic judgment. But that everything which is rational is therefore also actual (and thus exists) does not follow, for how could one comprehend that rationality must necessarily exist?[108]

On the basis of the distinction made in *Enc.* BC. § 6 between the concepts actuality and appearance, Hegel gives an explanation of the dictum in the *Preface* of the *Philosophy of Right* which caused so much trouble and aroused the suspicion that he was defending an arch-conservatism.

In a somewhat haughty fashion, Hegel expresses his amazement that people could so misunderstand him. Paragraph 13 of the *Preface* had already stated that the dictum expressed nothing but a conviction held by "every spontaneous consciousness".[109] *Enc.* § 6A repeats this by referring to religion and in particular to the religious dogma of divine providence. Religion is namely the concrete way in which the naïve consciousness, not yet formed or misformed by science and philosophy, is aware of the universe and its meaning. The religious belief that the world and its history are in God's hands expresses the fundamental conviction that the existence and the course of the universe is thought, brought forth and guided by a Spirit who is perfectly rational. One cannot believe in God's providence and at the same time believe that existing reality is fundamentally meaningless and wrong. Evil exists, too, and many phenomena could be different than they in fact are, but this does not mean that the heart of creation is not good and necessary. In the Christian belief, creation and redemption are the key words for the conviction that reality is an image of God and that evil is in principle vanquished. To this extent, religious consciousness is the certainty that whatever exists is rational and in Hegel's sense also actual. Although according to Hegel this consciousness is genuinely convinced that *everything that exists is fundamentally rational and thus actual*, with a lot of good will and admitting the ambiguity of "actual" (*wirklich*), one can also accept the sentence "What is actual, is rational" as a translation of religious consciousness.

But to what extent does religion also imply that "everything which is rational" is also "actual" (realized, existing rationality)? Rationality which necessarily exists is an idea that cannot be understood as not existing, a concept the realization of which is one of its essential moments. This unity of concept and existence is what Hegel calls "Idea". The necessity of this unity is expressed in the history of philosophy in the ontological proof for the existence of God. The highest thought, the concept of a perfect being, is not an abstract idea or "powerless" ideal, but the highest thinkable essence (thus absolute spirit), which necessarily exists. The true Idea realizes itself in the world of nature and spirit and in history, in which spirit develops and perfects itself. This fundamental philosophical idea corresponds to the religious belief in God's omnipotence, through which he can and will realize what he sees in his omniscience as rational. In its highest and most original form, reason is self-actualization.[110]

According to Hegel, what is paraphrased here is evidence of a religious consciousness. But it is also found in the philosophical consciousness. Hegel names two basic philosophical ideas which must be comprehended to correctly understand the dictum in question.

The first idea is a three-part idea, concerning God but therefore also concerning the reality of all that exists: 1) God is actual (according to the given definitions this means at least that God exists and is rational); 2) God is the most real (he is rational and existent to a higher degree than anything else; he is the highest rationality, which exists of itself and is the foundation and end of all other existence and rationality); 3) God is the only being of which one can say in all truth that it is actual (as the foundation of all other realities God is the only one who is real originally and of himself; all other realities have derived their actuality from God).

What does this concept of God have to do with the quoted dictum? If "actual" is taken in the sense indicated by Hegel, involving necessity and rationality, the second sentence of the dictum is a tautology, and we do not need the detour by way of God to understand it. If one understands "actual" more broadly and vaguely, as synonymous with "all that exists", then the affirmation of God as the rational ground of existence implies that all which exists (having its foundation in God) is rational. It is probably the latter that Hegel intends, notwithstanding his protest after the fact. The first sentence ("What is rational, is actual") is by no means tautological, but if God is not only "powerful" enough to make himself exist with everything that is implied in his rationality and also a being the existence of which is necessary, then the rational (*das Vernünftige*) is necessarily *real* (rational *and existent*). The conformation of God's existence implies the confidence that reason prevails and reveals itself in the reality of world and history.

The second philosophical thesis which one must know in order to understand the reciprocal implication of the rational and the actual is the difference between reality and appearance which has already been discussed. Both exist, but under appearance we find both the world of contingencies (chance, lotteries, ephemeral phenomena) and the world of errors and other forms of evil. Every reality has two sides: it is *real* in the strongest sense of the term (and thus rational and necessary) and at the same time an *appearance* (thus laden with contingencies and not immune to evil, and so possibly misformed or a caricature of itself or its idea). Reason can even understand that the contingent (thus the not-necessary and not deducible) and evil (i.e., the irrational and anti-rational) as such exist necessarily, but not why the particular factual contingencies and errors occur in the way they do.[111] Appearance is an essential part of the real; reality cannot exist unless it be in unity with all kinds of contingent phenomena. These comprise its "superficial exterior", but are not less real for that reason. God, rationality and reality are not possible without contingency. But a philosopher makes the greatest mistake if he sees contingent phenomena as being the most important. His superficiality puts an end to the thoroughness of true thinking, i.e., to the thinking of *reality*.[112]

True thinking, which understands the fundamental identity of rationality and reality, is compared in Hegel's remark to *Enc.* BC 6 to three inadequate ways of knowing the factual situation.

Ordinary *feeling* already suspects the difference between genuine reality and contingent facts or occurrences which "actually" did not have to happen.

The *imagination* conceives of philosophy and rationality as unreal mental creations which are much too perfect to be "true" and lack the strength to realize themselves.

The intellect, as faculty of differentiation, cannot see the basic coherence constituting the reality of fact and remains at the level of an analysis of the phenomenal. This analysis irrevocably becomes critique, for there is but little understanding or "prudence" (*Klugheit*) needed to discover objects, institutions and conditions which do not precisely correspond to their ideas and thus are not in *fact* what they ought to (*sollen*) be.[113] The criticism supplied by the intellect is sensible and correct, also in the political realm which it particularly loves to criticize. In certain periods, and for particular groups within the state, this type of criticism of political and other institutions (e.g., the church) is of great importance. The discrepancy between universal determinations which spring forth from the nature (or idea) of the matter (e.g., of legislation, government, property, the right to one's own opinion) and the factual realization of those matters cannot be skipped over. Criticism of fact in light of the true notion of the matters concerned plays a positive role in the improvement of institutions and conditions. In the *Philosophy of Right* Hegel himself exercised this sort of criticism sparingly, but it follows immediately from a comparison of the morality he thematizes and the historical facts of his time.

However correct the criticism of the understanding might be, it *is not philosophy*. At best it is based on philosophy, but as a consideration of the surface it does not reach the heart of the matter. Philosophy consists in an insight which does get to the heart of the matter: to its idea, which is realized in the (partly inadequate) phenomena, even if this realization is imperfect or even misformed. Or in the words of the *Philosophy of Right*: the philosophical concept penetrates through the outer surface[114] at which consciousness initially remains and gets down to the rational core (or "inner pulse"), and only then discovers that "the infinite wealth of forms, shapes and appearances" (in spite of all possible criticism) does indeed have its being thanks to that core and its dynamic.[115]

The train of thought presented here is once again and above all a plea for the second half of Hegel's dictum: what exists is much more rational than it seems to the eye and to the intellect. That "the rational, which is synonymous with the idea" (*Preface*, par. 13) also necessarily realizes itself (and that the inadequate forms will make way for adequate ones) is a presupposition which is expressed (e.g., by the sarcastic remark that the world did not wait for the intellect to create something good), but this presupposition is not argued for in either *Enc.* BC 6 or paragraph 13 of the *Preface*.

The quintessence of Hegel's notion of "reality" and its relation to rationality (or "Concept") and *Dasein* was also to be found in the Remark to the first section of the *Philosophy of Right* following after the *Preface*.

The true concept of something, in this case right, is neither an abstract concept (*blosser Begriff*) in the style of Wolffian rationalism nor the mere factual situation (*zufälliges Dasein*) confronting one. It is rather the *idea* of right, i.e., the unity of its concept and its existence: the concept of right which necessarily realizes itself (as a moment of the absolute Idea which causes its own existence, as is understood in the ontological proof for the existence of God), or in other words the *actuality* of right, which in spite of, and thanks to, its contingent and ephemeral exterior is the realization of reality itself. Cut loose from the concrete concept, the outward manifestation (appearance) of right changes into something unreal, incomprehensible, irrational, untrue and merely apparent. But as the expression of the idea of right, on the level of spatio-temporal contingency, this outward manifestation shares in the idea's rationality, even if it does so as a distortion or mistake. "The reason of an object" (*Grl.* § 2) is the concept of that object which necessarily gives itself reality. A true comprehension of this concept thus implies that one also understands its being-actual or the shape in which it is realized (*Gestaltung*) as a necessary moment *of the concept.* The form of the spatial and temporal *Dasein*, which is essential for this appearance (*Grl.* § 32) – and therefore for the concept – is thus a part of right's idea or rationality. Abstract concepts of the intellect concerning right, on the other hand, float above empirical reality and exhaust themselves in variations on an imperative "ought", a viewpoint in which the existing right is only an insubstantial, deceptive sham.

That the affirmation "this state is bad" does not always or necessarily reflect philosophical or civic incompetence, however, can be seen both from the fact that *all* political systems past *and present* are in Hegel's view to a greater or lesser extent deficient, and from such statements as the following: "A bad state is one which merely exists; a sick body exists, too, but has no genuine reality. A hand which is cut off still looks like a hand, and still exists, without being real."[116]

With the help of the preceding explanations paragraph 13 of the *Preface* can be read as follows:

Philosophy, like the naïve consciousness, proceeds upon the basic convictions 1) that reality (in the sense of "the existing") is meaningful, rational and thus comprehensible, at least generally speaking and in its foundations, and 2) that Meaning (what is rational in itself) necessarily realizes itself. *Energeia* and *Noëton* are two coextensive elucidations of *to on*. "Thought and being are the same."[117] Reminding us of what was said in paragraph 7, Hegel once again emphasizes that this "belief" in the fundamental rationality of existence is concerned not only with nature but also with the spiritual universe. The beginning of philosophy is thus the consciousness that recognizes the reason by which it itself is governed in the presence (*Gegenwart*) of the existent; it is an immediate acceptance of and radical agreement with factual reality. This consciousness changes when it distances itself from the present in the form of a feeling or reflection, which soon becomes critical. This distance arises unavoidably, for, as Hegel argues elsewhere, thinking implies a critical reflection on the nature and structure of the reality one confronts, and this reflection presupposes a distance between thinking consciousness and the objective order considered by it.[118] Reflection and distance are not only unavoidable, they are also essential moments of "the right of subjectivity": the individual has the right (and thus also the duty!) to know *himself* what is and is not rational in the actuality he experiences.[119] In sofar as consciousness sets itself up against the objective order in the intellect's reflection it is "subjective" and has the identity of subject and object with which it began behind and beneath it. This separation can already express itself on the level of feeling; in that case it is much less philosophical because feeling cannot justify itself by means of distinctions and abstract notions as the intellect can.

The distance by which the intellect is separated from the naïveté of the unprejudiced consciousness is a necessary and good phase in the process of thinking about right and state. The critical elements of its reflection can also be justified. The separation of consciousness and objective fact must however be condemned, as it is absolutized. The thinking of the intellect, which is *correctly* "beyond the present", may not remain at this "beyond". The transcending of the initial unity with reality is merely a phase: the negation it implies must be overcome by a return to actuality, in which it plays a subordinate role.[120] By not proceeding past the separation one necessarily falls into an attitude of mere criticism. Since the distance prevents the subjective consciousness from recognizing its own rationality in the objective order, it becomes dissatisfied and exhausts itself in supercilious and moralistic declamations about the difference between the world as it is and the world as it ought to be. This criticism, which would be partially true if it did not have the pretention of speaking the absolute and complete truth, is a symptom of the subjectivism and unreality in which feeling and understanding result when they are unable to comprehend the radical unity of subjective rationality and the rationality of existence. By separating itself from reality as it exists, the reflecting consciousness loses itself in unreal abstractions and unfulfilled demands. It does not thereby prove that reality is senseless or meaningless, but is itself negative and vain (*eitel*).

The negative attitude of this empty consciousness is caused by its superficiality. Due to its remaining on the level of phenomenal exteriors, it cannot see that they are *only* exteriors, in which a significant core is manifested. Every theory of state and right includes criticism based on an "ought" (*Sollen*) – the "ought" given with the idea of state and right which is seldom or never adequately realized. A true theory incorporates this criticism of the phenomena in a more radical explanation of the rational core or substance which realizes itself in the phenomena in spite of their contingency and temporality (and in spite of their inadequacy, possibly not mentioned here due to fear). One can criticize and improve everything from the outside, but that has nothing to do with philosophy. Of course concrete political and ethical life demands a number of positive laws, measures and decisions, but how these in fact occur in the concrete circumstances of a certain place and time is not a question for the philosophy of right.[121] Although the text suggests that justified criticism can only concern unimportant and indifferent matters, a philosophical concept of the state should also involve a critical examination of its *essential* elements, as it is also found in Hegel's philosophy of right. But such a critique is given on the basis of a fundamental agreement with the rational quintessence of the existing state, without which rationality no state and no critique of state would be possible. This agreement, the philosophical recovery of the identity of objective and subjective rationality, is Hegel's way of realizing what Spinoza called *amor intellectualis Dei*. An example of this is found in the following passage from the sketch of a letter quoted above, in which Hegel offers his book on the philosophy of state and right to the prime minister Hardenberg: "that my scientific striving aims at separating from philosophy that which unjustly usurps this name and rather at proving the *accordance* of philosophy with those principles which the nature of the state *needs*, most immediately however at proving its accordance with that which under his [majesty the king's] enlightened government and your wise direction of the Prussian state (to which for that very reason I am especially happy to belong) has already *in part* been achieved and which *in part* has the good fortune of *being achieved*."[122]

Paragraph 14 (p. XXI)

> This book, then, containing as it does the science of the state, is to be nothing other than the endeavour to apprehend and portray the state as something inherently rational. As a work of philosophy, it must be poles apart from an attempt to contract a state as it ought to be. The instruction which it may contain cannot consist in teaching the state what it ought to be; it can only show how the state, the ethical universe, is to be understood.

In paragraphs 12 and 13, with which the second part of the *Preface* began, Hegel indicated generally how philosophy must be related to existence. Paragraph 14–19 work this out with reference to the philosophical science of the state.[123] Paragraph 14 is presented as a consequence of the unity of rationality and reality (in the sense of existing reality) formulated in paragraphs 12–13. If it is true that what exists is fundamentally rational, one does not have to go beyond existence to discover what is rational; if that which is in itself rational (the idea) is also strong enough to realize itself, any theory which presents it as a Utopia is abstract and not completely true due to its ignoring the ideal's reality. Although the true theory of state is a theory of the true state, i.e., of the state as it actually *ought to be* in truth, according to its idea, and although Hegel himself thematizes the "ought" as an essential moment of the state in the *Philosophy of Right*[124] and as an essential moment of all reality[125] in the *Logic*, he says here, incorrectly and against his better judgment, that a philosophical treatise on the state must *in no way* construct how a state *ought to be* but "not at all" (*am entferntesten*) and "rather" (*vielmehr*!) how the factual state existing here and now must be known, i.e., understood. Hegel uses here the polemical and dualistic language of the thinkers of the intellect whom he condemns so strongly. Instead of his No to a normative and critical elucidation of the actual state he should have openly worked out and defended it as an element of his theory – one which is necessary according to the basic tenets of his own system. But if he had done so he might have had difficulties with the censor or have been threatened with dismissal. The fear of such unpleasant consequences was however not the only or the primary motive for Hegel's undialectical polemic here and elsewhere against the defenders of the "ought". By the end of his youth, in which he himself had been such a defender of the "ought", Hegel came to the following "*Resolution*" (!): "Strive, attempt more than today and yesterday! You will not be more than your time, but you will be it in the best way!"[126]

Paragraph 15 (p. XXI–XXII)

Ἰδοὺ Ῥόδος, ἰδοὺ καὶ τὸ πήδημα.
Hic Rhodus, *hic* saltus.

> To comprehend what is, this is the task of philosophy, because what is, is reason. Whatever happens, every individual is a child of his time; so philosophy too is its own time apprehended in thoughts. It is just as absurd to fancy that a philosophy can transcend its contemporary world as it is to fancy that an individual can overleap his own age, jump over Rhodes. If his theory really goes beyond the world as it is and builds [an ideal] one as it ought to be, that world exists indeed, but only in his opinions, an unsubstantial element where anything you please may, in fancy, be built.

Just as was paragraph 13, paragraph 15, too, is the exegesis of a sort of dictum. Hegel quotes it according to a fable ascribed to Aesop, bearing the title *The Braggart*, which runs as follows:

> A participant in the pentathlon whose achievements were always criticized by his fellow citizens as being insignificant once went abroad. After some time he returned and boasted that he had

> accomplished wondrous things in various cities, but that in Rhodes especially he had made a jump which could not be matched by any winner of the Olympics. He would have any of the witnesses attest to it, if ever one came here from Rhodes. But one of those present interrupted him, saying: 'But my dear fellow, if that is true you don't need any witnesses at all, for Rhodes is here, and here you can jump!' This fable makes clear that every word is superfluous if one had handy a proof through deeds.[127]

The key sentence of the fable in Greek is: "*αὐτού γὰρ Ῥόδος καὶ πήδημα*" or – in another version – "*Ἴδου ἡ Ῥόδος, ἰδοὺ καὶ το πήδημα*.[128] Perhaps Hegel is also thinking of the moral of the story, which he does not quote, in which the storyteller speaks of "*ἡ δι' ἔργων πεῖρα*", which is very similar to the *experience* or the empirical aspect (*ἐμπειρια*) of actuality (*ἐν-έργεια*) to which Hegel continually refers in the *Preface*. The word *πρόχειρος*, which is translated here as "handy", could be related to the present (*Gegenwart*), which is the concrete presence of the idea.[129]

The explanation Hegel gives is a new formulation of the second sentence of the riddle with which paragraph 13 began. "*What is actual*" (par. 13) is replaced here by "what is" (par. 15). Both are said to be "rational" or "reason". "What is", however, refers to beings or *Daseiendes* – to that which immediately presents itself and is experienced as factually existing (and thus not to the "reality" defined in *Enc.* BC 6A). How can Hegel say that "what is" (the existent, involving all sorts of contingencies, evils and malformations in addition to the realization of the idea) is the same as reason? He can only maintain this if he regards "what is" in a very specific way, *viz.* *as* the realization of the true idea, *as* "actuality" (i.e., *rational* reality), which it also is, in spite of its irrational elements. Only from this perspective can Hegel say that the existent is also necessarily rational. This statement, however, is either a tautology (*viz.* if we must analyse it to mean "what is" is rational *to the extent* that it is actual – and thus rational) or the immediate formulation of a postulate stating that the given must be intelligible, at least in its foundations. Even if we must understand the statement as a tautology it expresses the same postulate.

In Hegel's view, then, existence is the same as reason itself for speculative thinking. "This-here" (the Aristotelian *τόδε τι*) *is* true actuality (*το τί ἦν εἶναι* of the *ὄν*). That is why philosophy's task consists in the analysis and understanding of the here-and-now in its own necessity and rationality, and not in the constructing of an *other* actuality. Philosophy is the science of the true reasons behind what exists. By understanding the factually existing world in its factual "being-thus ', one at the same time makes clear why it must be as it is. It answers reasons demands; its "being" (*Sein*) agrees with the "ought" (*Sollen*) proclaimed by reason. Through understanding, the existent (*Daseiende*) is transformed into a genuine actuality (*Wirklichkeit*).

This is not to say that being and the "ought", factuality and ideality, are in tandem at every moment in world history. If this were the case, history would not even be possible, since the perfect identity of fact and ideal would leave no room for improvement. Hegel has shown in his philosophy that all preceding states and worlds have only been partial realizations of the true idea of state and world. Could he mean that his own time means the end of this partial realization? This seems improbable. Nor does it agree with what is said in paragraph 15 – and certainly not with what is said in paragraph 19. Hegel does not say that actuality is perfectly good and rational in all respects; he does not deny that the state as well as the idea and the philosophy of the state can be and must be improved. But he does argue with the view that an *individual* can spring beyond the political and cultural actuality of his time. When an individual philosopher criticizes and argues against his time and the world around him in function of a conceptual world which is not even potentially part of the factual culture, his mental image represents only a contingent and individual opinion and not a real possibility for the time in which he lives. But one can show that all philosophies, even the most "original" and extraordinary, are in some way the result of a more universal, super-individual consciousness: everyone, even the philosopher, is a "child of his time". For this reason one can even say (with some exaggeration and ignoring the individual styles characterizing original philosophers) that "philosophy" (that of some specific individual or of certain currents in a certain country at a certain time) is nothing but a mental whole in which and through which a certain time understands itself: "its time apprehended in thoughts". The point of Hegel's statement is thus directed against that individuality which disconnects itself from the cultural and historical context in which it lives. Whoever raises himself above the political and philosophical realizations of his time and wishes to pass judgment from a super-temporal viewpoint, like a god, is a braggart: he overestimates his possibilities and takes a contingent opinion (which at best is an expression of his own time) for an eternal truth. True criticism, a normative judgment of the factual political situation in the name of an idea of the state "as it ought to be" is possible, but not by means of an individualistic fantasy. It is possible only through the working out of an "ought" which is already involved in the factual situation of the (idea of the) state realized (partially and imperfectly) here and now. This is why Hegel can say elsewhere that a great man is not distinguished by a totally individual vision, but by his expressing and realizing what animates his time: "Whoever expresses the wishes of his time, stating them and accomplishing them, is the great man of that time. He does what is the inner core (*das Innerste*), the essence (*das Wesen*) of the time, and realizes it...".[130]

The motivation behind Hegel's polemic against a *certain* form of "ought" philosophy is thus here again his rejection of every subjectivistic individualism. He ridicules the pedantic doings of those who replace philosophy with emotional and capricious fantasies and then raise these to the standards against which they measure the world in their vanity. His criticism must be read against the background of his criticism of subjectivism in *Grl.* §§138–140A.[131] The "vanity" evidenced by the contested "philosophy" is not only a theoretical but also a moral vice. This also explains Hegel's scornful tone.[132]

Paragraph 16 (p. XXII)

With hardly an alteration, the proverb just quoted would run:

Here is the rose, dance thou *here.*

Hard reality – the solid, empirical ground on which true philosophy stands and finds the truth – is the actual world. But this Rhodes of philosophy is a hard reality in another sense as well. As shall be stated in paragraph 17, the actual state of the world is a painful one: a cross. Philosophy recognizes this, but understands this cross in such a way that it is transformed into a harmony. Rhodes (*Rhodos*) then changes into a rose (*rhodon*), in which philosophy can find joy. Its jumping or springing (*saltus, saltare*) is thereby transformed into a sort of jubilation over the reason concealed in reality: one does not need to flee the here and now, but can dance where one finds oneself. This dancing is freed of all trammels (according to paragraph 17 it is no longer subject to "the fetters of some abstraction or other") because it now recognizes the rose *in* the cross.[133]

Paragraph 17 (p. XXII)

> What lies between reason as self-conscious spirit and reason as existing actuality, what separates the former from the latter and prevents it from finding satisfaction in the latter, is the fetter of some abstraction or other which has not been liberated [and so transformed] into the concept. To recognize reason as the rose in the cross of the present and thereby to enjoy the present, this is the rational insight which reconciles us to the actual, the reconciliation which philosophy affords to those in whom there has once arisen an inner voice bidding them to comprehend, not only to dwell in what is substantive while still retaining subjective freedom, but also to possess subjective freedom while standing not in anything particular and contingent but in what is in and for itself.[134]

With the metaphor of the rose and the cross Hegel is alluding to both the heart of Christian belief and the symbolism of the Rosicrucians. The latter allusion is stressed by Hegel himself in a review which he wrote in 1829.[135] He makes it understood there that one would have to be quite "ignorant" in order to miss this allusion. It takes on particular meaning if R.K. Hočevar, basing himself on H. Hattenhauer, is correct in writing the following:

> The connection of this Hegelian symbolizing of reason with a rose and the ALR [i.e., the moderen Prussian law: the *Allgemeines Landrecht für die Preussischen Staaten* of 1794, which replaced the old and old-fashioned legal system] can only be realized when one knows that the king's advisers who were opposed to the ALR – especially Johann Christoph von Wöllner – belonged to the secret order of the Rosicrucians. The latter attempted to achieve 'knowledge of the final things, the mysteries' in the sign of the rose by 'means of mysticism, theosophy, magic and alchemy.' 'Cool, clear, enlightened *ratio* [of which the ALR was a result] was opposed to the flight into irrationalism as a confession of faith. The corresponding battle against the Enlightenment – and thus against the work of the reformers of justice, however had already been waged 'when the Rosicrucians succeeded in admitting the then-crown prince and later King Friedrich Wilhelm II into the order'.[136]

In a veiled manner, then, Hegel could be understood here to be directing himself to the king and his reactionary advisers with the message that true philosophy, expressed in the *Philosophy of Right*, does precisely what they wish: it legitimizes the reconciliation and satisfaction with the existing political reality by showing that it is as beautiful as a rose – in spite of its painful aspects. The fact that Hegel is not on their side, however, but on the side of the modern, post-Napoleonic legal state and thus a defender of the ALR, choosing in favor of the group of enlightened ministers such as Hardenberg and Altenstein, is clear from the main text of the *Philosophy of Right*, but not from the *Preface*. This lack of clarity and the appearance of agreement with the Rosicrucians among the politicians are tricks employed in Hegel's rhetoric. According to Lasson and Löwith,[137] Hegel is also alluding to Martin Luther's coat of arms, in which he summarized his theology in a symbolic fashion. Although this coat of arms also combines the rose and the cross (but also the heart), and although it might seem evident that Hegel is trying to show here, as he so often does, that his philosophy is in complete agreement with the content of the true faith, his interpretation, which fits the symbol of the Rosicrucians perfectly, seems to have another representation in mind than Luther's. Luther describes his representation as follows: in a heart which has maintained its own, living (i.e., red) color, a black cross stands, one which gives pain and dies off, but does not kill. The heart is situated in the middle of a rose, coloured white to symbolize joy and the comfort of faith. The rose is standing in a sky-blue field (its white is the beginning of the future joys of heaven) and encircled by a golden ring (to indicate that heavenly joy lasts for all eternity and surpasses all other joys).[138] The text around it reads, "The Christian's heart is borne on roses, even when standing beneath the cross."[139]

But even if Hegel did not have Luther's symbolism in mind, it is as good as certain that he wanted to express the identity between his philosophy and Lutheran theology here. The words "cross" and "reconciliation" have all too clear a theological connotation. The reconciliation achieved by the association of the cross with the resurrection to eternal life is confirmed by speculative thought and translated as the unity of reason and its own hard reality. Rose and cross thus become metaphors for the concept and the various forms of division and evil conquered by the concept. It is in this sense that Hegel notes with reference to section 3 of the *Philosophy of Right* that "one may believe that a legal system and legal order can exist which [...] is *purely rational* [...] one demands that it *should* be so [... This demand] is correct, but also incorrect. – Correct is [:] reason should be the ruling element, and is so in a developed state – in general [reason] does [rule in the state] – [it is] more rational than one might think [...]; [the] present appears to reflection [and] particularly to self-conceit [,] as a cross ... [but] the rose – i.e., the reason in this cross is introduced by philosophy".[140]

The opposition between ideal and fact is discussed in the same way in the lectures on the *Philosophy of Religion*. The following passage clearly alludes to the Lutheran imperative, "Take up your cross!", and presupposes the traditional Christian symbol of the crucifix, which bears fruit for eternal life: "The ideal of the state is quite correct, only unrealized [...]. That by which the ideal is determined can be at hand, but it is not yet recognized that the idea is actually present, for the latter is considered only by finite consciousness. It can be known even through this covering (*Rinde*) of the substantial heart (*Kern*) of reality, but hard work is needed to this end; to pluck the rose in the cross of the present one must take up the cross oneself."[141] It is striking in this last sentence that Hegel parallels the opposition of rose and cross with that between "covering" and "heart" or "core", which played such an important role in paragraph 13. The whole passage of the *Philosophy of Religion* can be read as a summary of Hegel's conception of the coherence between *Sein* and *Sollen*, *fact* and *ideal*, *core* and *surface*, *essence* and *appearance*, *good* and *evil*, passion, patience and felicity.

Lasson is correct in referring in his commentary on paragraph 17 to the end of Hegel's article "Belief and Knowledge" (*Glauben und Wissen*), where a speculative explanation of God's death and resurrection is given.[142] The cross and God-forsakenness which we must bear is the seeming incomprehensibility of factual history; eternal life, however, consists in the insight that it is fundamentally necessary and divine.

Lasson also refers to a passage from Hegel's essay "Who thinks abstractly?" The passage reads, "Christians may well practice Rosicrucianism, or rather Crucirosism (*Kreuzroserei*), and encircle the cross with roses. The cross is the long-sanctified gallows and rack. It has lost its one-sided meaning, as the tool of humiliating punishment, and represents instead the greatest pain and deepest rejection together with the greatest joy and divine honor".[143] The image which Hegel has in mind here is not only different from Luther's coat of arms, it is also different from the Rosicrucians symbol, on which the preceding paragraphs are based. The symbol of a cross encircled by roses is rather, as Lasson also remarks, reminiscent of Goethe's fragment *Secrets*, which also alludes to the Rosicrucian symbolism. In this fragment, "the sign ... which is a comfort and hope for all the world" appears to Brother Mark as a "cross tightly wound in roses".[144]

In philosophical language, not metaphorical but conceptual, Hegel explains the reconciliation with hard and painful reality as follows. "The present reality", of which "actuality" (*die Gegenwart*) consists, presents itself as a bad, unacceptable reality (a cross). The individual subject who sees himself placed in this reality and the universal self-consciousness of the present time as expressed in public opinion, literature and current philosophies cannot make peace with the world's condition. One feels trapped, subjected to a hostile reality. The cause of this lack of freedom however lies in an attitude and optic on the subject's part: the abstract, unspeculative way in which the subject regards reality, not moving past its contingent and particular aspects, not penetrating to the core which unfolds within it but is not identical with it. Philosophy teaches another optic: an insight which penetrates down to the core of reality and understands painful phenomena as the particularization or contingent play of a substance in itself rational. This optic and attitude are no longer abstract, as is the case with the reflective understanding which only sees contradictions; they are rational and thus concrete. The thinking subject's rationality meets the rationality of reality as it is *in and for itself*. Concrete freedom, satisfaction and joy result from the unity of reason in the form of the self-conscious spirit *and reason in the form of* present reality. The substance of the present and the subject who thinks about it coincide in the one Reason which realizes itself in the reconciliation of both. Their unity presupposes a distinction between the heart of reality on the one hand ("what is in and for itself") and particular contingencies on the other. If one looks at the particular and contingent alone (an abstract approach, outside the truth) they do indeed represent evil and meaninglessness; as the manifestation of essence however they are seen to be the workings of Reason.

With this explanation Hegel has solved the riddle of the dictum with which paragraph 13 began, which says that the rational and the actual imply one another – at least if we may read the dictum as follows: Reason has two modes of existence 1) in the form of a rational subject who thinks in a rational way (R^1), and 2) in the form of a reality which is in and for itself rational and actual (R^2). R^1 and R^2 are identical, because and to the extent that they are both actualizations of one and the same (rational and real) Reason. *Via* and in their essential foundation they imply one another.

Paragraph 18 (p. XXII–XXIII)

> It is this too which constitutes the more concrete meaning of what was described above rather abstractly as the unity of form and content; for form in its most concrete signification is reason as conceptual knowing and content is reason as the substantial essence of actuality, whether ethical or natural. The known identity of these two is the philosophical Idea. – It is a sheer obstinacy, the obstinacy which does honour to mankind, to refuse to recognize in conviction (*Gesinnung*) anything not ratified by thought. This obstinacy is the characteristic of our epoch, besides being the principle peculiar to Protestantism. What Luther initiated as faith in feeling and in the witness of the spirit, is precisely what spirit, since become more mature, has striven to apprehend in the concept in order to free and so to find itself in the present. The saying has become famous that 'a half-philosophy leads away from God' – and it is the same half-philosophy that locates knowledge in an 'approximation' to truth – 'while true philosophy leads to God'; and the same is true of philosophy and the state. Just as reason is not content with an approximation which, as something neither cold nor hot, will be spewed out, so it is just as little content with the cold despair which submits to the view that in this earthly life (*in dieser Zeitlichkeit*) things are truly bad or at best average, though here they cannot be improved and that this is the only reflection which can keep us at peace with the actual world: There is less chill in the peace with the world which knowledge supplies.[145]

The identity of the subjective and substantial reason illuminated from various angles by paragraphs 13–17 is translated by Hegel at the beginning of paragraph 18 with the help of the pair of concepts with which his discussion on method began (par. 3 – section 11). The logical (and in that sense abstract) categories *form* and *content* were introduced in paragraph 3 to make a definition of the true method possible. Philosophical method is not a form applied externally to a certain content, for the form and content of truth are one: a philosophical notion is nothing but the unfolding in thought of the matter thought of.

The more concrete realization of the logical form (realized in the natural and spiritual reality) is reason in the form of conceptual knowledge (i.e., of the free subject treated in paragraph 17); the concrete content is the substance discussed in paragraph 17: the substantial essence of (natural and spiritual) actuality. True reality, the truth which comes to light in philosophy, i.e., the philosophical Idea, is the identity of form and content (as was stated in paragraph 4) or (as we can say after paragraph 17) the identity of the comprehending *subject* (R^1) and the comprehended reality or *substance* of nature and spirit (in particular, that of the ethical) (R^2).

After the inclusion brought about by Hegel's reference back to paragraphs 3–4 which rounds off his argument, Hegel returns to a point briefly touched on in paragraph 6. This point is presupposed throughout but is suppressed by his polemic against the self-conceit (*Eigendünkel*) of the pseudo-philosophers who are always in opposition. In paragraph 6, Hegel recognized in passing the "high" and "divine" right of man to liberate himself through a cognitive examination of factual ethicity; in paragraph 5 it had already been made clear that the thinking subject can be content with no single authority but must examine all givens in the search for a conceptual justification which can enable him to attain inner peace. Paragraph 18 formulates this right to free thinking even more clearly. Hegel even declares that the demand for understanding is nothing other than a more adult form of the *sola fide* on which Luther based religion and the whole meaning of existence.

In contrast to the vanity of the self-conceit which Hegel has argued against in this *Preface*, he now praises the "independence" which reveres nothing and recognizes no authority whatsoever unless it is first justified by thought. What is incomprehensible deserves no obedience. This independence, thematized in part two of the *Philosophy of Right* (especially sections 129 ff.), is characteristic of the "more modern period" (i.e., of the time from the Renaissance to Hegel). It is the distinguishing principle of Protestantism, which is itself the only true interpretation of Christianity.[146] What Luther made the basis of all knowledge and life on the level of feeling and under the name of "faith" is in Hegel's view the same as the experience of the philosophical concept by which the subject is reconciled with reality and thus liberated.

The clear affirmation of this right to free thinking can appear to be a conciliatory gesture toward theologians and semi-philosophers, against whom Hegel was so vitriolic in the first part of the *Preface*. In the passage immediately following however, Hegel again puts them in their place by making a distinction between a "half" searching for cognitive justification and a radical search for the same. The relativists who despair of the possibility of discovering truth and those who consider an *approach* to truth at best possible are examples of a "half philosophy". With their understanding they go only half the way which must be travelled. As seen in paragraph 7, they end up with an "atheism of the ethical world". It is also with reference to them that the dictum is applicable that a half philosophy leads away from God (and the truth concerning the state), while a complete or true philosophy – the radical thinking which goes beyond the intellect's reflection and replaces it with speculative (i.e., conceptual) rationality – leads to God and the truth of the state). The latter makes a true and warm peace with reality possible, due to its showing that reality is fundamentally rational and that one can join in with it heart and soul. The intellect's half philosophy at best achieves an acceptance of reality for lack of better.

The dictum quoted by Hegel here probably goes back to Francis Bacon, who wrote in *De dignitate et augmentis scientiarum*, "It is very certain and has been shown in experience that a slight taste of philosophy easily leads to atheism, while deeper imbibing leads back to religion".[147] Leibniz quotes this idea of Bacon's at least three times, *inter alia* in his *Confessio naturae contra atheistas*: "Francis Bacon of Verulam, a man of divine rationality, has said correctly that a passing tippling at philosophy leads away from God, while a philosophy drunk to the bottom leads back to him".[148] Hegel's quotation is more similar to this last sentence than to Bacon. As Hegel points out, the dictum had become a common expression in his time; in the version he quotes he could have used it without having to know the first person to have expressed such a thought.

That Hegel declares the applicability of this dictum concerning the relation of God and philosophy to the relation of philosophy and state can be explained by his conception of the state as the objectivity of spirit, which as absolute spirit is God. As the reality of the ethical Idea, the state is divine, in a sense which must be further specified.[149] The mistake of the "atheism of the ethical world" is that it only superficially understands the state and does not recognize God's work in it. In this way it remains only half way along on the way to God.[150]

Paragraph 19 (p. XXIII–XXIV)

> One word more about giving instruction as to what the world ought to be. Philosophy in any case always comes on the scene too late to give it. As the thought of the world, it appears only when actuality is already there cut and dried after its process of formation has been completed. The teaching of the concept, which is also history's inescapable lesson, is that it is only when actuality is mature that the ideal first appears over against the real and that the ideal apprehends this same real world in its substance and builds it up for itself into the shape of an intellectual realm. When philosophy paints its grey in grey, then has a shape of life grown old. By philosophy's grey in grey it cannot be rejuvenated but only understood. The owl of Minerva spreads its wings only with the falling of the dusk.

Hegel returns once again to the critical and Utopian philosophies which oppose the present reality in the name of high ideals to which that reality does not correspond. By way of a later explanation of the final sentence of paragraph 14, the positive part of which was commented on in paragraphs 15–18[a] (philosophy is the knowledge of the factual ethical universe), Hegel explains why a philosophy that wants to teach us how the state or world "ought to be" not only reveals all the mistakes and vices indicated in paragraphs 3–11 but also necessarily comes too late to do what it intends.

As the "thought" or concept of the actual, empirical and historical world which must be given in experience before it can be comprehended, philosophy is itself an exponent of the world and time which are brought to an understanding of themselves in that philosophy. That a world is reflected in the form of a transparent and coherent system proves that its realization has been completed. Its "presence" is a present perfect, the now of a self-knowledge separating an accomplished completion from a new time and world to grow out of a new, as yet uninaugurated principle. The philosophical transcription of a historical world is *objective* spirit realized here and now – the objective spirit which comprehends itself (as *absolute* spirit) by means of individual subjects (*subjective* spirit) who are part of its reality and intuit and comprehend it in its truth. The "ideal world" (*das Ideale*) which thus arises (absolute spirit, which differentiates itself in art, religion and philosophy) is a mirror in which the objective world of right and morality recognizes its essence and meaning. As long as objective reality is still "unfinished", laden with inconsistencies, faulty expressions of its principles and remainders of a previous period, no all-encompassing concept of it is possible. A philosophical system which represents its full truth presupposes that it has already come to complete fruition.

The intellectual realm, into which philosophy transports the substance of the objective world, gives a precise rendition of the foundation of that world. But both are still differentiated from one another by an "over against". Not only because the real (the content) and the ideal (the form) as such are not the same, but also because the highest perfection of the world – just as the flourishing of plants and animals – is at the same time the transition to that world's decline and death. The greyness of its notions (Hegel is alluding here to Faust's "Grey is all theory"[151] is the color of old age and death. Philosophy is at one and the same time the celebration of a high point in history and a *meditatio mortis* at the dying of a world realm. Philosophy is not prophecy but a remembrance. The owl of wisdom begins its flight at the moment when dusk falls.[152]

A good illustration of paragraph 19 is found in Plato's philosophy, treated in paragraph 12.[153] Plato wanted to teach the people of his time, especially the politicians, how the state "should be". As has been said, however, his political philosophy was nothing other than an extravagant expression of his time, also and particularly in those elements through which he argued against the new principle of subjectivity. The *Republic* contained the internally inconsistent reality of the ancient *polis* and the destructive principle of subjectivity inaugurated by Socrates. Plato's love for the old *polis* that no longer existed and his rejection of the new principle drove him to a Utopia which he tried to introduce in opposition to the spirit and the style of his time. His impotence was made evident, however, by his becoming unjust and violent in the process. Only true reason, which would ascend (par. 12) but needed time to do so, could combine the old and new principles harmoniously. And it was only many centuries after the introduction of this harmony of principles by Christ, only after it had been developed and worked out in the objective reality of society in right, morality and state, only through Hegel's philosophy that it was possible to understand fully why and how society must be ordered on the basis of the two basic principles of antiquity and Christianity.

With paragraph 19, therefore, Hegel lets us know that his philosophy of right is also a conclusion and that the state he describes there is not a state of the future but the end of a past history. It is true that he suggests various improvements for the existing states in Europe in the *Philosophy of Right*, but these are part of the latest completion of the idea of the modern state described here. They are moments of the latest appearance produced by world history to this point, but the death knell has already sounded for it. The period characterized by Hegelian morality is in principle already finished. Just as there was a long period of transition between Plato and Christ, so, too, is it possible that the state legitimized by Hegel will last for centuries; a new foundation is not yet in sight and cannot yet be philosophically thematized. The thinker has to wait to see what history gives him to think about. Experiences are not constructed, they are acquired. And without experience no truth is possible.[154]

Paragraph 20 (p. XXIV)

> But it is time to close this preface. After all, as a preface, its only business has been to make some external and subjective remarks about the standpoint of the book it introduces. If a topic is to be discussed philosophically, it spurns any but a scientific and objective treatment, and so too if criticisms of the author take any form other than a scientific discussion of the thing itself, they can count only as a subjective epilogue and as arbitrary assertion, and he must treat them with indifference.[155]
>
> Berlin, June 25, 1820.

Hegel's final comments state that the genre of the *Preface* which they bring to a close is unscientific, and announce that the writer will respond only to scientific and not to purely subjective criticism.

The style of the *Preface* is called "external" and "subjective" here. In the preface to the second edition of his *Encyclopedia* Hegel characterizes the genre of the preface as an "exoteric" way of speaking.[156] And elsewhere we read, "In the *Logic*, as in the *Encyclopedia*, it is said time and again that in *Prefaces* and *Introductions*, i.e., *before* science, one speaks in a historical (*historisch*) and "reasoning" (*räsonnierend*) way, and not scientifically".[157]

If we take Hegel literally, philosophy would have to be as indifferent to the content of this and all of Hegel's other prefaces as Hegel declares himself to be here concerning all of the subjective and chance assurances which his philosophical work can call forth. The claims made in the text which has been so extensively analyzed here prove nothing. In themselves they give us no insight into reality. Yet the text is overflowing with philosophical elements which are scientifically analyzed and deduced in their proper places in Hegel's works. The goal of this commentary was to show the pre-philosophical significance and internal connection of the *Preface* of the *Philosophy of Right* and a number of relations through which it is bound up with Hegel's philosophy so clearly that one can read this text as an initiation into the truth of Hegel's thought.

NOTES

1. The *Preface* is quoted here following a division into 20 paragraphs. The dictum *What is rational* ..., which is on p. XIX of the original edition, is counted here as part of the following paragraph (13) and the lines ᾿Ιδοὺ Ῥόδος ... on p. XXI as part of the paragraph following them (15). References to page numbers follow the original edition. The English version of the *Preface* is taken from T.M. Knox's translation in *Hegel's Philosophy of Right* (Oxford University Press, London-Oxford-New York 1952[1]). In this admirable translation I have changed a few expressions in accordance with my commentary which was written on the basis of the German text as found in J. Hoffmeister's edition (Hamburg, Meiner 1955, 1967[4]).
2. Cf. par. 12 (p. 86): "In the course of the following treatise *I have noted* ..." (italics mine). The reference is to § 185.
3. The expression "external and subjective" (par. 20) will be explained in the commentary to par. 20.
4. The term "immediate knowledge" (*das unmittelbare Wissen*) is not used in this Preface, but functions in the Berlin versions of the *Encyclopedia* (BC. 61–78) as a title for a sort of philosophy, best exemplified by Jacobi, to which the philosophers criticized in this *Preface* also adhered. The extent to which Hegel is also referring to Schleiermacher here would have to be researched. Cf. Note 28 above.
5. Cf. also Riedel's characterization of the literary genre of the *Philosophy of Right* in M. Riedel (ed.), *Materialien zu Hegel's Rechtsphilosophie* I, pp. 17–20.
6. I translate both *Grundriss* (Knox: "manual") and *Kompendium* by "compendium", *Leitfaden* (Knox: "text-book") by "guide" and *Lehrbuch* (Knox: "compendium") by "text-book". Knox's text has been changed accordingly.
7. These marginal notes were first published by J. Hoffmeister in his edition of the *Philosophy of Right* (Hamburg 1955, pp. 301–430); K.H. Ilting has published a more precise version of them in the second volume of the *Vorlesungen über Rechtsphilosophie 1818–1831*, pp. 81–629. They refer to §§ 1–180 of the *Philosophy of Right.*

8. Cf. F. Nicolin, "Ein Hegelsches Fragment zur Philosophie des Geistes", in: *Hegel-Studien* I, p. 9 ff.
9. The various editions of the *Encyclopedia* are referred to here with the letters A (for 1817), B (1827) and C (for 1830), following F. Nicolin and O. Pöggeler (see their edition of the third edition, Hamburg 1959, p. 466). The sections are referred to by the number after the letter: A. 400; B. 562; C. 319; BC. 299.
10. I am reserving a comparison of the philosophy of right in the *Encyclopedia* and that in the *Philosophy of Right* for a complete commentary on the latter.
11. I have changed Knox's "enlarged" (for *weitere*) to "more extensive".
12. Knox translates *meinem Amte gemäss* by "in the course of my personal duties".
13. This paragraph was split into two paragraphs by Knox.
14. I have changed "their" (guiding principle) to "its" (*darin*), "classification" (for *Einteilung*, which is the German translation of the traditional *divisio*) to "division", "recognized" (for *erkannt*) to "known" and "manual" (for *Grundriss*) to "compendium". Instead of "discursive thinking" I would prefer "intellectual thinking" or "the intellect's thinking" to render *Verstandeserkenntnis*, but such a translation would presuppose a general agreement on the translation of *Verstand* and *Vernunft* as "intellect" and "reason".
15. The method is the all-inclusive pure form of the (onto)-logical universe: *Logik* II (ed. Lasson), pp. 483–506; *Enc.* A. 184–189.
16. Here we see for the first time the terminology and problematic which so fascinated the young Hegel (1789–1800). See A.T.B. Peperzak, *Le jeune Hegel et la vision morale du monde*, The Hague 1969[2], pp. 15–25, 52–55, 80–82, 93–101.
17. Hegel's philosophy of feeling is perhaps his Achilles' heel. Except for a number of sections in the *Encyclopedia* in which he thematized diverse forms of feeling, it is contained in a large number of remarks characterized by a strongly polemical tone and an almost compulsive stereotyping.
18. Cf. par. 6–8, and particularly the quotation from Goethe on p. XII: "Do but despise intellect and knowledge..." (*Verachte nur Verstand und Wissenschaft*).
19. In the editions of the "Philosophische Bibliothek" (Hamburg, Meiner) the *Phänomenologie des Geistes* contains 564 pages, the *Encyklopädie* of 1830 463, the *Logik* 904 and the *Rechtsphilosophie* 297.
20. Hegel's wish that his works be judged primarily for their "logic" (par. 3: "It is also from this point of view above all...") has not been fulfilled. See my commentary below on par. 20 and M. Riedel in *Materialien zu Hegels Rechtsphilosophie* I, pp. 17–40.
21. This commentary on the *Preface* to Hegel's philosophy of right is a preliminary study for a commentary on the body of the work in which the primary concentration will be placed on the logical structure of Hegel's views. A part of this, *viz.* the analysis of §§1–32 and 142–156, was presented at the colloquium on Hegel's philosophy of right held in September, 1979 in Fontenay-aux-Roses and published in two parts: "Zur Hegelschen Ethik", in: D. Henrich and R.P.

Horstmann (eds), *Hegels Philosophie des Rechts*, Stuttgart 1982, p. 103–131, and "Hegels Pflichten- und Tugendlehre", in: *Hegel-Studien* 17 (1982), p. 97–117.

22. Cf. Luke 16, 29–31. Which predecessors does Hegel mean here by "Moses and the prophets"? His comparison with the biblical founders of religions is reminiscent primarily of the great ancients of philosophy, such as Plato and Aristotle, and perhaps Descartes, Spinoza and Kant. Against this one could argue that the philosophy contested in this passage is scarcely able to understand the speculative thoughts of its great predecessors, let alone embody them. Leibniz and Wolff are even greater predecessors who according to Hegel also think in an unspeculative manner typical of the intellect. They have transmitted Aristotelian theories in a modern, not very intellectual manner. That Hegel is probably thinking primarily of them here seems to be confirmed by a text from April 16, 1822 of Hegel's concept for a *Gutachten* (a critical evaluation), in which he uses this kind of expression. He writes there that the many handbooks on philosophy which are published every year "are [either] a scanty repetition of the ancients or one expanded with useless additions", and he adds: "According to my humble view the entire style and purpose of this instruction would involve the teacher's being referred to the old textbooks of the Wolffian school and in simply plugging the Kantian table of categories in for the Aristotelian one in the proper place" (*Berliner Schriften*, p. 553, Note 3).
23. It is very difficult to translate Hegel's *Sittlichkeit*. The adjective *sittlich*, which I will always render by "ethical", is in Hegel's thought by no means synonymous with "moral" (*moralisch*). Morality (*Moralität*) and "Ethicity" (Sittlichkeit) are related as the abstract or formal structure of the good and its concrete actuality in the life of a human community having its appropriate institutions. "Ethical life" and "Ethics" do not render the full meaning of *Sittlichkeit*. I will use (and abuse) the ugly, but faithful word "ethicity".
24. The first sentence of this paragraph in Knox's translation reads: "After all, the truth about Right, Ethics and the state is as old as its public recognition and formulation in the law of the land in the morality of everyday life, and in religion". The truth is much older than its public recognition by the law. "Morality" (for *öffentliche Moral*) is adequate, but I want to reserve this word for the translation of Hegel's *Moralität*, which has a very different meaning (see the preceding note). Probably *öffentlichen* belongs also to *Religion*: the publicly recognized Christian (principally Lutheran) religion agrees with the old truth about law, morals and politics. – I have replaced "untrammelled thinking" (for *das freie Denken*) by the more fundamental "free thinking" in order to preserve the close relationship between thought and freedom.
25. Cf. Hegel's discussion of empiricism in *Enc.* C. 37–39; 61–78 and his *Vorlesungen über die Geschichte der Philosophie* III (Werke XV; Glockner 19), pp. 278–296, 417–439, 493–500.
26. This is a summary of the way in which Hegel grounds his philosophy of the objective and the absolute spirit and of his view concerning "the experience of consciousness" which the individual acquires through education as a "child of his time" and "heir" to a cultural history.

27. Notwithstanding the impression which Hegel's system, and in particular his *Encyklopädie*, can create, his philosophy is not a construction of the universe on the basic of a most abstract nothingness. It is, rather, a *re*construction and *re*production which attempts to match the reality confronting us with a thinking *re*creation of it.
28. Although the "ought" is not the final word in philosophy, it does constitute an essential moment of all truth and reality. This explains its key role in the logic of being and the concept, in the philosophy of the subjective practical spirit, and in the philosophy of objective spirit. Cf. *Logik* (ed. Lasson) I, pp. 119 ff.; II, pp. 304 ff.; *Enc.* C. 233–235; 470 ff.; 507 ff.; *Grl.* §§129 ff.
29. Cf. below the commentary on paragraph 13 and the discussion of Hegel's identification of "actuality" (*Wirklichkeit*) and "rationality" (*Vernünftigkeit*).
30. It appears that neither the word *Kultur* (culture), which is used by Herder, nor the word *Zivilisation* (civilization) is used by Hegel in any of his works.
31. This short summary of Hegel's view on the meaning of culture and history is an anticipation of a complete interpretation of his philosophy of history and his philosophy of the objective and absolute spirit. All of the presuppositions formulated under a) through f) are just as much the *results* of Hegel's philosophy (i.e., of my interpretation of that philosophy) as they are presuppositions.

    In a manuscript on the philosophy of world history dating from 1830 (*Die Vernunft in der Geschichte*, pp. 28–30), Hegel writes that the philosophical consideration of history has only one presupposition, *viz.* that the world is governed by reason (*die Vernunft*) and thus that history has progressed rationally. This presupposition has been proved by philosophy, in those parts of it which precede the philosophy of history. It can be explained in four moments: 1) Reason is the *substance* of natural and spiritual life and activity: i.e., "that in which all reality has its being and existence." 2) Reason is the *infinite power*, not a mere ideal or "Ought" found outside reality – God only knows where, or if it is only in the minds of some idealists. 3) Reason is the *infinite content* of all natural and spiritual life; i.e., the essence, truth and true matter on which thinking reflects. The latter needs no material other than itself. Philosophy is impossible without experience, but the truth of the empirical ("true experience") is nothing other than concrete rationality here and now. 4) Reason is also the *infinite* form of thought; i.e., the activity by which it forms, orders and comprehends the content of nature and spirit. Philosophy proves that only the Idea is the true, eternal and unconditional or absolute power which reveals itself in the world. The world reveals nothing other than the splendor of the Idea. But to discover the rationality of the world and its history one must be in possession of reason and rationality oneself: "Whoever looks at the world rationally is looked at rationally by the world as well" (*idem*, p. 31, cf. also pp. 32 and 259).
32. Cf. R. Koselleck, *Preussen zwischen Reform und Revolution*, Stuttgart 1975[2] and R.K. Hočevar, *Hegel und der Preussische Staat*, München 1973.
33. Cf. *Grl.* §§243–245.
34. E. Gans already pointed out in his preface to the second edition of Hegel's

Philosophy of Right (1833) that the jury verdict, the publicness of the verdict and the class parliament did not exist in the Prussia of his time. Cf. *Materialien zu Hegels Rechtsphilosophie* I, p. 245. K. Rosenkranz observes later in his *Apologie Hegel gegen Dr. Haym* (1858): "But Hegel cannot have copied the Prussian state of that time, for he taught the necessity of the constitutional monarchy, popular representation, the equality of all citizens before the law, the publicness of judicature, the jury and the freedom of public opinion. Did these institutions exist in Prussia? No. Knowing this, how is it possible to maintain that Hegel based his philosophy of right and state on the model of the bureaucratic Prussian police state?" See M. Riedel, *Materialien zu Hegels Rechtsphilosophie* I, p. 401. In his biography of Hegel (*Georg Wilhelm Friedrich Hegels Leben*, 1844, pp. 332–334), Rosenkranz had also listed a number of institutions, some modern, some out of date, which were not yet or no longer to be found in Prussia during Hegel's time but which were present in Hegel's philosophy of right (*inter alia*, the bicameral system, public debates to prepare legislation and majority rule). In his book *Hegel als Deutscher Nationalphilosoph* (Leipzig 1870) Rosenkranz writes: "It is all the more incomprehensible that anyone could read any servility on Hegel's part toward the Prussian government in it [i.e., Hegels' Philosophy of Right], as if he had simply copied how the empirically given Prussian state was in its various divisions. Hegel was not untrue in Prussia to the notion of state which he has defended in Baden against the Württemberger reaction. At that time Prussia was not governed by a constitution; it provided for no publicness or verbal character of judicature, no freedom of the press, no equality of citizens before the law, no part played by the people in legislating or allowing taxation – and Hegel taught that these are all philosophical necessities". P. Landau points out in an article on "Hegels Begründung des Vertragrechts" (in: *Materialien zu Hegels Rechtsphilosophie* II, pp. 176–197) that Hegel's conception of contractual obligations not depending on delivery does not agree with Prussian law at that time but with the *Code civil* (p. 189).

35. *Briefe* II, pp. 241–242 publishes the draft of a letter from Hegel to Prime Minister Hardenberg which must have been written in October of 1820. Although Hegel says there that his "official duty" required him primarily to fulfill a scientific and theoretical task, he also seems to be indicating in a cautious and veiled manner that his philosophy of right could be of significance "not only for the schools" but also for the government: "I knew ... that my scientific striving aimed at separating from philosophy that which unjustly usurps this name and rather at proving the accordance of philosophy with those principles which the nature of the state *needs*, most immediately however at proving its accordance with that which under his [majesty the King's] enlightened government and your wise direction of the Prussian state (to which for that very reason I am especially happy to belong) has already *in part* been achieved and which *in part* has the good fortune of *being achieved.* – My treatise will accordingly be an attempt to deal with the major characteristics of what stands before us in its tremendous efficacy, the fruits of which we enjoy, and I do not think I presume too much when I maintain to this end

that philosophy, in performing this task proper to it, justifies the protection and favor received from the state, and that in its limited sphere of influence, which nonetheless reaches that which is innermost in man, it can effect an immediate *promotion of the government's beneficent goals*" [my emphasis]. Cf. also the draft of a similar letter from Hegel to Altenstein in *Briefe* II, pp. 237–238.

36. Cf. Plato, *Gorgias* 502 ff. (on rhetoric as flattery) and the *Republic* 562a ff. (on the relation between tyranny and flattery).
37. The image of Hegel as the official and influential state philosopher is thus a total fabrication.
38. Plato's demand for "rendering an account" (λόγον διδόναι) becomes for Hegel the possibility and necessity of the concept.
39. With an allusion to the epistle from the apostle Paul to the Romans, in which he writes: "The same spirit bears witness to our spirit, that we are God's children", Hegel gladly cites the "witness of spirit", but understands it in a secularized sense. Cf. e.g., *Religionsphilosophie* (ed. Lasson) I, p. 94: "Spirit bears witness to spirit. This witness is the proper inner nature of spirit. In it is found the important condition that religion lies ... in man ... himself, in his reason and freedom". See also *idem*, pp. 96, 289, 290, 298. In a purely "ethical" sense the "witness of spirit" also figures in *Grl.* §147. The connection between both meanings of the "witness of spirit" is indicated in paragraph 18 of this Preface: "What Luther initiated as faith in feeling and in the witness of the spirit ..."
40. Cf. *Historisches Wörterbuch der Philosophie* I, 1031–1032. From Aristotle and the Stoics via Cicero (who introduces the term *consensus*) through the English common sense philosophy of the 18th and 20th centuries, this has always been an important notion.
41. Cf. e.g., *Enc.* C. 71 A; *Religionsphilosophie* II (*Werke* XII; Glockner 16), pp. 401–403.
42. This paragraph is split into two paragraphs by Knox. I have changed his translation "what is publicly accepted as truth" (for *die öffentlich bekannte Wahrheit*) to "the publicly accepted truth", whose ambiguity is exploited by Hegel in connection with his use of the words *gültig* (valid) and *geltend* (actually accepted and maintained). Whereas *gültig* is a normative expression, *geltend* does not pronounce a judgement about the intrinsic value of the existing laws. Instead of "valid", used by Knox for both expressions, I have preferred "maintained" for *geltend*. I did not change Knox's "ethical order" as translation for *Sittlichkeit*, but, in order to maintain its wide meaning, I have changed "ethical life" into the ugly, but more adequate neologism "ethicity". For the same reason *etwas Besonderes* is not rendered by "some *particular* character", but by "something particular".
43. Cf. *e.g. Grl.* §§185+A; 352–359.
44. Cf. *Grl.* § 147: the "feeling of self" (*Selbstgefühl*), which coincides with the "witness of spirit" (cf. Note 39) expresses a relation between the individual subject and the existing rational order which is "even more identical than *belief* and *faith*". Cf. also *Grl.* §257.

45. According to the introductory sections 1–32, the general definition of right is "the existence of freedom" (*das Dasein der Freiheit*). The more specific definition of freedom, which is important for paragraph 6 and the entire *Preface*, is thematized in sections 132 and 137A called an "honorable obstinacy" in paragraph 18.
46. Cf. paragraph 9, in which "hatred of law" is called the sign of vicious ideas and attitudes concerning morality.
47. Cf. *e.g.* paragraph 9.
48. Cf. *Enc.* A. 112–114 and *Logik* II, pp. 239–264.
49. Cf. Hegel's verse *Entschluss* from 1801: "Kühn mag der Götter Sohn der Vollendung Kampf sich vertrauen, / Brich denn den Frieden mit mir, brich mit dem Werke der Welt! / Strebe, versuche du mehr als das Heut und das Gestern! So wirst du / Besseres nicht, als die Zeit, aber auf's Beste sie sein!".
50. Cf. *Enc.* 75–91; *Logik* II, pp. 129–136; 156–169; 477–483.
51. In this paragraph the following changes have been made: *Geist* has been translated as "spirit" (Knox: "mind"); "a new and particular" (*eine neue und besondere* [*Theorie*]) replaces "a special and original"; "the result is that if the ethical world is Godless..." (for *dass nach diesem Atheismus der sittlichen Welt*) has been changed into "the result of this atheism of the ethical world is that"; instead of "empty reflection" I prefer "vain reflection" to render *Reflexion und Eitelkeit*, and *absprechen* seems to me to be weaker than "condemn", more like "criticize".
52. Here, for example, the passages from Hegel's *Geschichte der Philosophie* referring to the ancient world at the time of Socrates and the Stoics would have to be analyzed, as well as those concerning the "barbarism" of the Middle Ages and the poor contemporary situations in the "Roman" countries, England and Turkey. Cf. also *Grl.* §3A (p. 13): "quite correct; Roman family law, slavery, etc. do not satisfy even the slightest advances of reason".
53. Cf. *Grl.* §138A: "As one of the commoner features of history (e.g. in Socrates, the Stoics, and others), the tendency to look inward into oneself and to know and determine from within oneself what is right and good appears in ages when what is recognized as right and good in the ethical actuality cannot satisfy the will of better men. When the existing world of freedom has become faithless to the will of better men, that will fails to find itself in the duties there recognized and must try to find in the ideal world of the inner life alone the harmony which actuality has lost". Notice *nicht... kann* ("cannot") and *muss* ("must").
54. Although Hegel's argumentation here seems to identify "the ethical world" with "the spiritual universe", it is all too clear from his philosophy that the world of spirit is broader and includes art, religion and science. An identification of the state with morality as such is made impossible by Hegel's course of thought as it is expressed e.g. in *Grl.* §30A and the division of the third section; but Hegel made it so often nevertheless that one does not have to explain it away in the paragraph of the *Preface* in question here either.
55. In an early letter to Schelling (April 16, 1795), Hegel still writes: "With the spread of the ideas of how things *ought* to be, the indolence of settled people

to eternally accept everything as it is will disappear" (*Briefe* I, p. 24). In Frankfurt Hegel begins to have a higher opinion of *Being* and after Jena he criticizes the moralism expressed in various absolutizations of the *Ought*. Perhaps Hegel was influenced in this transformation by Spinoza, who concerning the morality of the philosophers says in §1 of the first part of his *Tractatus Politicus*: "homines ... not ut sunt, sed, ut eosdem esse vellent, concipiunt". This idea was also already to be found in Machiavelli's *The Prince*, section XV.

56. I do not know to which epistemology Hegel is alluding with the word "problem". Cf. however Kant, *Kritik der reinen Vernunft* A.256 (= B.311): "ist selbst ein Problema"; A.328 (= B.384): "so bleibt es ein *Problem* ohne alle Auflösung"; B.392: "lediglich ein reines und echtes Produkt, oder Problem, der reinen Vernunft"; A.338 (= B.396): "keine Kenntnis, obzwar einen problematischen Begriff".

57. Cf. the places cited in Note 44 and *Grl.* §268+A, where the "patriotic" inclinations of the citizens are discussed as being the "substantial foundation" of the state. A clear commentary from Hegel himself on the sentence "because ultimately this is the position of everybody" can be found in Ilting III, pp. 724–725. Hegel gives the following explanation of *Grl.* §268 there: "This conviction [that my substantial and particular interest is contained and maintained in the interest and purpose ... of the state] is held to a greater or lesser degree by everyone, without his knowing it, no matter how much people may cast aspersions and complain. For if you take hold of them and ask them earnestly if they would wish that all of what they complain about did not exist, they would retreat from this position and come to the awareness that the basis of their entire existence is and can only be the state, and that it must therefore be maintained ... The early stages of cultivation always begin with finding fault, and later always seek the positive in everything... The apparent political inclinations must therefore be distinguished from what people genuinely want. They want the state inwardly, although they are not always aware of this, but they do not go beyond particulars and are pleased with themselves in this vanity and know-it-all attitude of wanting to understand". Cf. a similar commentary in Ilting IV, pp. 642–643: "The spirit of a nation continues on in every individual whether he knows it and fights against it or is unaware of it, as one eats and drinks without knowing about anatomy. In his particular being, in his actions, that spirit is the driving and the unmovable element in him which brings him to act. No matter how much people rationalize about their time and their state, they are still fully a part of that time and state in which they have their foundation; if these were taken away, these people would fall into a vacuum, and to that extent they have more trust than they themselves and others believe... It is difficult to determine to what extent people are serious in their rationalizing, finding fault and being dissatisfied; they can carry on and become vehement, but the extent to which this is really serious people do not know themselves."

58. *Grl.* §§316–320 treat public opinion and censorship. See my commentary in "Der Staat und Ich", in: *Hegel-Jahrbuch* 1975, pp. 83–104.

59. *The Sophist* 261 a 7; cf. also *Theaetetus* 180 c 5.
60. This paragraph was split into two paragraphs by Knox. I have translated *Gegenstände* by "topics" (Knox interprets them as "institutions"), kept "his own" (*den Seinen*) instead of translating with Knox " the elect", eliminated the quotationmarks from the topics of Fries' speech, and translated *Wahrnehmung* by "perception", not – as Knox does – by "sense-perception", because it refers in this context to an immediate knowledge of the heart and not to one or more of the five senses. The sentence in which Hegel compares Fries c.s. with the "atheist" Epicurus is one of the many gramatically incorrect phrases that can be found in Hegel's work. Hegel does not want to say that Epicurus' cosmology is in fact a normative theory, but rather that the principle of his cosmology lies in contingency (*Zufälligkeit*). As the *Willkür* (the subjective faculty of choice or *liberum arbitrium*) is the contingent aspect of the will, the *ethical* view of Hegel's enemies can be compared to the *cosmological* view of Epicurus. In accordance with this interpretation I have changed Knox' translation, which reads: "According to a view of this kind, the world of ethics (Epicurus, holding a similar view, would have said the 'world in general') ....". Instead of "speculative thinking" (Knox) my "conceptual thinking" remains closer to Hegel's "dem denkenden Begriffe". In Goethe's text I maintained "science" (instead of "knowledge") for *Wissenschaft*. At the end of the paragraph I maintained Hegel's sequence of *Wahrheit und Gesetze*.
61. To whom is Hegel referring here with "recent philosophy" (*Philosophie der neueren Zeit*) (Knox: "recent philosophical publications"). In his courses on the history of philosophy, *Geschichte der Philosophie*, he uses the expression "the philosophy of modern times" (*die Philosophie der neuen Zeit, Werke* XV and Glockner 19, pp. 267) for philosophy beginning with Bacon und Böhme, but he also allows "philosophy" or "modern thought" (*das Denken der neueren Zeit, Werke* XV and Glockner 19, pp. 274 and 328) to begin with Descartes (cf. also *Werke* XIII, p. 129; Glockner 17, p. 145). Here, in paragraph 8 of the *Preface* to the *Philosophy of Right*, Hegel must be thinking of his contemporaries, who were on a level far beneath that of the modern political and legal philosophies of Hobbes, Grotius, Pufendorf, Rousseau, Kant and Fichte. Cf. *Geschichte der Philosophie* (*Werke* XV; Glockner 19), pp. 439–446, 526–529, 551 ff.
62. "He giveth to his own in sleep" ("Den Seinen gibt Er's schlafend") is a loose quotation from Psalm 127, verse 2: "Es ist umsonst, dass Ihr früh aufsteht [...], denn seinen Freunden gibt Er's schlafend" (It is vain for you to rise up early [...], for so he giveth his beloved [even in their] sleep).
63. Cf. Hegel's repeated criticism of the contemporary theology in its two forms: rational theology (*Vernunfttheologie*) and the theology of feeling (*Gefühlstheologie*). It is especially by the second, pietistic and undogmatic theology, strongly represented at the University of Berlin by Schleiermacher, De Wette, and Tholuck among others, that Hegel's polemic is repeatedly aroused. See *e.g.* the preface to the second edition of the *Encyklopädie* with the long note on Tholuck, *Enc.* BC. 573 Remark, and the *Philosophie der Religion* (ed. Lasson) I, pp. 35 ff.

64. Cf. what is said in the Introduction concerning Hegel's relation to Fries, De Wette and Schleiermacher.
65. The same thought is expressed in a similar context in *Grl.* §270A,e (pp. 261–262).
66. Hegel cites the first part of Goethe's *Faust* in which Mephistopheles, disguised as Faust, says immediately before the appearance of the student:

    Verachte nur Vernunft und Wissenschaft,
    Des Menschen allerhöchste Kraft,
    Lass nur in Blend- und Zauberwerken
    Dich von dem Lügengeist bestärken,
    So hab ich dich schon unbedingt! –
    Ihm hat das Schicksal einen Geist gegeben
    Der ungebändigt immer vorwärts dringt
    Und dessen übereiltes Streben
    Der Erde Freuden überspringt.
    Den schlepp ich durch das wilde Leben,
    Durch flache Unbedeutendheit,
    Er soll mir zappeln, starren, kleben,
    Und seiner Unersättlichkeit
    Soll Speis und Trank vor giergen Lippen schweben,
    Er wird Erquickung sich umsonst erflehn;
    Und hätt er sich auch nicht dem Teufel übergeben,
    Er müsste doch zugrunde gehn!

    By leaving out ten lines and changing the first two and the last two lines, Hegel changes the meaning of these verses. In the *Phänomenologie des Geistes* (GW 9, p. 199) Hegel adapts them in the following form which, except for the person, corresponds for the most part with the version in the *Philosophy of Right*:

    Es (a certain form of self-consciousness)
    verachtet Verstand und Wissenschaft
    des Menschen allerhöchste Gaben –
    es hat dem Teufel sich ergeben
    und muss zu Grunde gehn.

    Evidently Hegel is quoting from memory in both works, as he did with the psalm quoted in Note 62 and the line from Aesop's Fables cited in paragraph 15. He apparently remembered the quoted texts in the version given in the *Philosophy of Right.*
67. Cf. on this point A. Peperzak, "Religion et politique dans la philosophie de Hegel", published in: G. Planty-Bonjour (ed.), *Hegel et la Religion*, Paris 1982, p. 37–76.
68. Cf. *Grl.* §§28–29 with reference to the word "objective" which Hegel uses repeatedly in an ambiguous sense in the *Philosophy of Right.*
69. Cf. e.g., *Geschichte der Religion, Werke* XIV (Glockner 18), pp. 70–122, *Philosophie der Religion* (ed. Lasson) IV, pp. 142 ff.
70. Cf. *Grl.* §30A.
71. Besides changing "mind" (for *Geist*) to "spirit" and "ethical life" (for *das Sittliche*) to "the ethical", I have changed "justice" (for *Recht*) to "right"

and the more elegant "private hearth" (for *Partikularität*), which, however, obscures the opposition between the universality of the law and the particularity of subjectivistic feelings, to the very literal "particularity". *Die Form des Rechten* (in which expression *das Rechte* has to be heard as a substantivally used adjective, synonymous with "the good") has been translated as "the form in which the right appears" (Knox: "the formal character of the right").

72. In accordance with the scholastic distinction between *universale, particulare* and *singulare*, "singularity" (*Einzelheit*) must be taken here in a neutral sense which is synonymous with "individuality".

73. Cf. *Le jeune Hegel et la vision morale du monde*, pp. 11–28, where Hegel's vocabulary in Tübingen is also studied, in particular on pp. 12 and 16–17.

74. In §258A (pp. 245–246 of the original edition in the footnote), to which the phrase "as I have remarked somewhere in the course of this text-book" refers, Hegel also reproaches the conservative Von Haller with "the most bitter hatred of all *laws*". In this passage Hegel calls the "hatred of the law" "the shibboleth by which fanaticism, feeblemindedness and the hypocrisy of good intentions openly and unmistakably reveal themselves for what they are, [and] dress themselves in whatever guise they may". From this we see that Hegel's diagnosis and polemic, which appear in the *Preface* to refer only to Fries, are also applicable to another, restorative current in jurisprudence: the historical school of right represented by the conservative Karl Ludwig von Haller, who became a Catholic in 1820 and was therefore released from his important political functions. With this reference Hegel probably wanted to point out that he was not only distinguishing himself from the "progressive" but also from the "restorers", who proceeded on the basis of principles as bad as those of the former. Cf. also Hegel's excerpts from Haller's *Restauration der Staatswissenschaft*, in: *Berliner Schriften*, pp. 678–684.

75. A review from February of 1822 in the *Allgemeine Literaturzeitung*, published in Halle, reproaches Hegel with a malevolent interpretation of the speech by Fries quoted in paragraph 8. Cf. *Berliner Schriften*, pp. 750–751.

76. "Pursued as a private skill" (or art), instead of Knox's "pursued in private like an art" seems to me to be more faithful to *als eine private Kunst exerziert*; I have kept "science" for *Wissenschaft* (instead of "learning"), "the ethical" (not " the ethical life") for *das Sittliche* and "ethicity" for *Sittlichkeit*. I have changed "starts ... from" (for *führt ... auf*) to "leads ... to". The awkward expression *wird sich nicht etwa durch den Titel abweisen lassen, der..* (Knox: "Is not likely to suffer any diminution as a result of") has been changed to "cannot be denied by". Instead of "ultimate source" the German text reads *substantielle Quelle* ("substantial source") and "what is deserved" (for the vaguer *gehörte*) I have changed to "all right".

77. Hegel's consciousness of his practice of philosophy as an official duty in service of the state is made evident by various letters. Cf. *Briefe* II, pp. 237–238 ("Proof of my official activity" and "rendering an account..."): pp. 241–242 ("my official obligation"); *Berliner Schriften*, p. 751.

78. Cf. *Grl.* §270A.

79. Cf. pp. 328–329 of the original edition of the *Grundlinien*.

80. In *Grl.* §§138A (and supplement); 274 + supplement and 279, Hegel compares his time to that of Socrates. Cf. also the marginal note at §138A (Ilting II, p. 491: "Viewpoint of the abstract conscience... this is the major viewpoint and illness of our time. Solution – respect for the present objectivity of morals") and *Werke* XI, pp. 350–351.
81. Instead of "speculative knowledge" I have chosen "Conceptual knowledge" for *begreifende Erkenntnis; der physischen und geistigen Natur* (Knox: "nature and mind") is translated here by "the natural and spiritual world"; instead of "the laws of ethics" (*die Gesetze des Sittlichen*) the text adopted reads "the laws of the ethical". The beginning of the last sentence I would rather translate in the following way: "principles of the most criminal kind..." (*die verbrecherischten Grundsätze*).
82. Concerning the publications in the positive sciences Hegel is probably thinking particularly of Hugo (*Grl.* §3A), Von Haller (*Grl.* §§219A and 258A) and Savigny (whom he does not name, but who as leader of the historical school of right must have felt himself the target of Hegel's attack on Hugo). Theologians against whom Hegel polemizes are De Wette and Tholuck (see Note 63) and perhaps Schleiermacher.
83. Perhaps Hegel is thinking here among other things of Schleiermacher's plan to abolish the philosophical class of the Academy. See above, Note 10.
84. See Rosenkranz, *Georg Wilhelm Friedrich Hegel's Leben*, pp. 336–337 and *Berliner Schriften*, pp. 750–751.
85. The entire review is printed in Ilting I, pp. 461–474.
86. Rosenkranz, *op.cit.* p. 337. Cf. *Berliner Schriften*, pp. 750–751.
87. *Philosophie der Weltgeschichte* (ed. Lasson) pp. 771 ff.
88. Hegel argues that the pseudo-philosophical relativism that considers all convictions to be equally good is the same as the legitimation of criminal notions, in *Grl.* §140A:e (pp. 145–149).
89. Plato's analysis of tyranny (the *Republic* 565d ff.) probably also plays a role here. Anti-philosophy is ungrateful to pseudo-philosophy, which it contests and which is basically a form of violence. Cf. in this connection Hegel's analysis of subjectivistic morality in *Grl.* §140A, which also turns into an accusation of the violent anarchism it conceals.
90. Knox splits this paragraph into two.
91. "Which lives in the light of its consciousness of these" refers to the consciousness and "self-consciousness" (*Selbstbewusstsein*) which works in the government in a non-philosophical way and in the professors in a philosophical way. It is the task of the latter to make explicit and purify this consciousness on the part of the state.
92. Cf. above p. 56 and Note 28.
93. *Enc.* BC. 6A.
94. Cf. *Grl.* §140 and *Philosophie der Religion* (ed. Lasson) IV, pp. 102–109 and 121–129.
95. I hope to show this in a complete commentary on the *Philosophy of Right*. I believe I have already done this for sections 1–32, 105–141 and 142–156 in the studies quoted in Note 21.

96. Hegel's view of the difference between Socrates and Christ demands a separate study. Several indications are given in *Philosophie der Religion* II, *Werke* XII (Glockner 16), pp. 187 and 295.
97. Cf. *Grl.* §124A and many other passages such as §§162A, 206A, 228A, 236A, 260A, 262, 274, 290A, 301A, 316, 328; *Enc.* C. 540A.
98. *Grl.* §185A. Private property (§46 + A), the right to have a family (§162 + A) and freedom of choice of profession (§206A) are essential expressions of the principle of subjectivity. But Hegel scarcely thematizes the specifically political aspects of this principle.
99. Cf. *Berliner Schriften*, p. 336, where Hegel himself writes concerning the end of paragraph 12: "Here it is so explicit that a misunderstanding seems impossible: the principle of Christianity and the more abstract principle of infinite personality are indicated here explicitly as the principle to which Plato's nostalgy refers and around which the hinge of world history has turned". Cf. also what Hegel says about Plato's view of the relationships between right, philosophy and religion in *Enc.* 552A, pp. 436–438.
100. Cf. *Philosophie der Weltgeschichte* (ed. Lasson) III, pp. 644–647; *Geschichte der Philosophie, Werke* XIV (Glockner 18), pp. 100–117.
101. See Note 80.
102. The same course of thought is expressed in Hegel's discussion of public opinion, freedom of the press and censorship (*Grl.* §§308–320). A public discussion in the parliament or "Class Assembly" (*Ständeversammlung*, something that did not exist in Prussia) is necessary, just as is freedom of the press, in order to give "the people" a chance to take part in state affairs and to be satisfied with how they are conducted.
103. *Was vernünftig ist, das ist wirklich;*
und was wirklich ist, das ist vernünftig.
104. I did not make any changes in the text, except the replacement of "mind" by "spirit", but added some Hegelian expressions within parentheses.
105. Cf. *Logik* I, G.W. 11, pp. 369 ff.; *Enc.* BC§6 + A and §142 ff.; *Grl.* §1 + A.
106. The text of *Enc.* B 6 + A is identical to that of the third edition except for a couple of stylistic changes and three clear additions. The commentary given here is based on the third edition.
107. Cf. e.g., *Enc.* C. 6A: "every idea, error, evil", "just as every existence however troubled and transitory". Paragraph 13 of the *Preface* does distinguish between the foundation and the mass of contingent and external phenomena of which reality consists, but Hegel does not explicitly mention here any forms of evil, such as political and economic errors, corruption, injustice, reaction, intrigues, misuse of power, intolerance and so on. Did he want to prevent the censor from waking up? But cf. *Grl.* §§268Z and 270Z and *Briefe* II, p. 242 ("in part still to be achieved").
108. That this is Hegel's conviction appears e.g. from passages like these: "that which is and corresponds to its concept, is necessarily" (was ist und seinem Begriff gemäss ist, das muss sein", Wa. §44A, p. 50); "What is rational, must happen" ("was vernünftig ist, muss geschehen", Wa. §134A, p. 192; see also the end of the Remark); "What is rational becomes actual and the actual be-

comes rational" ("Was vernünft ist, wird wirklich, und das Wirkliche wird vernünftig", An, p. 51. Here "actual" is used as synonymous with "real" or "existent"). That this conviction does not exclude the possibility and the reality of a temporary divorce between reason and actuality (which may last a very long time!) follows from a statement of 1818: "Reason projects an ideal of the state [i.e.] its constitution, but the form of actuality is very different from it. – Universality belongs to the character of the rational. This is, however, still incomplete as long as the idea does not actualize itself" ("Die Vernunft entwirft ein Ideal des Staats, der Staatsverfassung, von dem die Gestalt der Wirklichkeit sehr verschieden ist. – Zum Charakter des Vernünftigen gehört das Allgemeine. Es ist aber noch unvollständig, solange nicht die Idee in die Wirklichkeit tritt". WH, p. 210–211). The authenticity of this passage is attested to by an almost identical note of Wanneman who followed the same course as Homeyer, from whose notes the above quotation is taken: "Die Verfassung entwirft ein Ideal des Staates, der Rechtsverfassung, von dem die Gestalt der Wirklichkeit sehr verschieden ist" (Wa, p. 270). Cf. also – with regard to the difference between the essential or universal right and positive law: "The positive law of all states conserves determinations which are not in accordance with reason" ("Das Allgemeine muss vernunftgemäss sein, die Autorität und Form machen das Positive der Gesetze aus. Eine solche Vermischung besteht in allen Staaten; es haben sich nämlich in allen nicht vernunftgemässe Bestimmungen in dem positiven Recht erhalten", Wa, p. 269). The philosophy of right is concerned with the *idea*, i.e., the true and universal ideal of right, morality and state; it is, however, neither an abstract, "platonic" ideal, nor a historicist glorification of the facts: "The philosophy of right neither stops at an abstraction nor at a historical perspective if this is not in accordance with the *idea*. It knows that the realm of right comes into being through a progressive evolution only and that it is impossible to skip any stage of this evolution" ("Die Philosophie des Rechts bleibt weder bei der Abstraktion noch bei der geschichtlichen Rücksicht stehen, wenn diese der Idee nicht gemäss ist. Sie weiss, dass das Reich des Rechtlichen nur durch fortschreitende Entwicklung entstehen kann und eine Stufe derselben zu überspringen ist". Wa, p. 206). Cf. also Ilting IV, pp. 632–633.

109. Knox translates *Jedes unbefangene Bewusstsein* as "the plain man".

110. On Hegel's version of the "ontological argument for the existence of God", cf. *inter alia Logik* I, G.W. 11 pp. 47–50; II, G.W. 12 pp. 127–131; *Enc.* C. 51 + A; 193 A and *Grl.* §280A, where the unity of concept and existence (*Begriff* and *Dasein*) which is expressed in the ontological argument and in which the "depth of the idea" consists is identified with the truth. Without this unity no knowledge is possible.

111. Cf. *Logik* I, G.W. 11, pp. 381–389; *Enc.* C. 145 *Zusatz; Grl.* §214A: "It is reason itself which recognizes that contingency, contradiction and mere appearance have their own, though limited, sphere and right, and it does not trouble itself with solving such contradictions".

112. As examples of juridical contingencies that do not fall under the competence

of philosophy Hegel quotes by heart and in a slightly distorted way passages from Plato's *Laws* VII, 789e–790a, and Fichte's *Grundlage des Naturrechts* §21 (*Akad. Ausgabe* I. 4, pp. 87–89). In the indicated passage Plato says that the lawgiver should not enter into details like that of taking a baby everywhere on the arm until the time he can stand on his own feet. Plato thus agrees with Hegel's view. Hegel's phrase *Plato konnte es unterlassen* could be translated in this sense: "Plato could, i.e., was justified, in omitting...", but the parallellism (*ebenso*) with Fichte, who indeed recommends putting a picture into the passports "of important persons" (a restriction neglected by Hegel) forbids such a translation.

113. Compare "This [philosophy] has to do only with the Idea, which is not so powerless as to consist only in an ought and not be real, and thus has to do with a reality in which those objects, arrangements, conditions, etc. are only the superficial exterior" (*Enc.* C. 6A, end) and *Enc.* C. 38A: "We find in empiricism this great principle, that whatever is true must be real and available to perception. This principle is opposed to the *Ought*, with which reflection inflates itself, belittling reality and the present in favor of a *Hereafter* which is to be found only in the subjective understanding. Like empiricism ... philosophy, too, only recognizes what *is*; it knows nothing of that which only *ought* to be and thus *is not*".

114. The metaphor of *die bunte Rinde* ("the motley covering") is used also in the Course on Aesthetics: "Die harte Rinde der Natur und gewöhnlichen Welt machen es dem Geiste saurer zur Idee durchzudringen als die Werke der Kunst". (*Werke* X^1, p. 14). A very helpful commentary on the opposition and *Aufhebung* of *Sein* and *Sollen* is to be found in *Enc.* §234 *Zusatz.*

115. Cf. *Die Vernunft in der Geschichte*, pp. 31–32: "In order [...] to recognize the universal, the rational [in the world and world history], one must oneself be rational [...]. If one takes on the world with subjectivity alone, he will understand the world to be as he himself is made up: he will always know better, see how things should have been done, how things should have occurred. Most of world history, however, is and must be rational; a divine will is the ruler of the world and is not so powerless as not to determine that history. [In order] to recognize this one must have the consciousness of reason [...] the eye of the concept, of reason, which pierces the surface and penetrates the manifoldness of the motley confusion of occurrences". In his course on the philosophy of right of 1819–1820 Hegel says that someone who feels unfree in the state should blame himself for it, for insofar as there is a state, and not an anarchic war of all against all, freedom has actualized itself as "concrete freedom": "Man has his highest freedom in the state, because in it the concept [of freedom] is an object [objective] for him. If a man does not know this, he must obey the laws as a servant. He can see the state's demands as an exterior constraint and gnash his teeth; that is his affair. It is his own fault and misfortune that he feels this way. He can also take refuge in complete resignation, but he remains [thus] always in complete dependency" (An, p. 226–227). In the *Zusatz* indicated in the preceding note Hegel characterizes the negative criticism with regard to the [social

and cultural] world as an attitude of the youth: "The youth believes that the world is in an absolutely bad shape and must be transformed completely". "The attitude of the adult" (*Die Stellung des Mannes*) includes the recognition "that the final aim of the world not only is accomplishing itself eternally, but also has accomplished itself" ("dass der Endzweck der Welt ebenso vollbracht is, als er sich ewig vollbringt"). The same criticism of the youth's criticism is found in Ilting IV, pp. 632–633. Cf. also *Grl.* §268 *Zusatz.*

116. Ilting III, p. 727. Cf. also Ilting IV, pp. 632–633: "The Idea of the state should not be understood as the thought of a particular state or particular institution; one must consider the Idea, this actual God. Although one may declare a state bad in light of one's own principles, and although one might find some deficiency in it, if the essential (*das Wesentliche*) is found in it, namely that, as a state, it is a Christian European state, then it must (*muss*) contain all essential moments of [the Idea of] the state". The most fundamental explanation of the unity in difference of actuality (*Wirklichkeit*), appearance (*Erscheinung*) and being (*Sein*) is given in *Logik* II, G.W. 12, pp. 173–178. On pp. 175–176 the structure of the Idea is illustrated through a consideration of the finite, the deficient, the bad and the dying state.

117. Hegel's confidence in the fundamental rationality of reality is coupled with a fundamental faith in the ability of human reason to figure out the secrets of reality. Cf. *e.g.* the famous words which Hegel spoke at his inaugural lecture in Heidelberg (cf. *System und Geschichte der Philosophie*, pp. 5–6) and repeated almost literally in his inaugural dissertation in Berlin: "... To begin with, however, I can demand nothing [of you] but that you bring with you a confidence in *science, faith* in *reason*, confidence *and faith in yourself.* The *courage of the truth, faith in the power of spirit* [is] the first condition of the *study of philosophy*; man must honour himself and *consider himself worthy of what is highest*. He cannot think highly enough of the greatness and power of the spirit; the self-contained essence of the universe *has no strength in itself* which could resist the courage of knowledge; it must open itself to knowledge, laying its riches and depth before its eyes and allowing its enjoyment" (*Berliner Schriften*, pp. 8–9). In the lecture with which Hegel began his course on the philosophy of world history on November 18, 1830 he formulated the rationality of empirical reality as follows: "The only idea intrinsic to philosophy [...] is the simple idea of *reason*, that reason rules the world, and thus that world history has progressed rationally." (*Die Vernunft in der Geschichte*, p. 28). What follows, *viz.* that this basic idea at the beginning of his course is a presupposition, but that it is *proved* in philosophy is a presupposition, but that it is *proved* in philosophy so that one no longer has to believe it but *knows* that it is true, can also be stated concerning the faith in one's own reason which Hegel asked of his students in the opening lectures of 1816 and 1818. "This conviction and insight is a *presupposition* with respect to history [or also: reality] as such. In philosophy itself this is not a presupposition; in philosophy it is *proved* by speculative knowledge that reason is [...] [1] the *substance*, [2] *infinite power*, [3] the *infinite matter* of all natural and spiritual life and [4] the

infinite form, and activating (*Betätigung*) of its content ... That such an Idea is the True, Eternal and All-powerful, that it reveals itself in the world and [that] nothing is revealed in it except itself, its splendor and its dignity, is what is proved in philosophy, as has been said, and what is therefore *presupposed* here as proved" (*ibid.*, pp. 28–29; cf. also pp. 38–39 and 258). The idea that the world is fundamentally rational is traced by Hegel himself back to Anaxagoras, who transmitted it to western philosophy *via* Plato (cf. *Phaedo* 97b–98b) and Socrates: "Historically Anaxagoras is said to be the first to state that *nous*, i.e., intelligence or reason, rules the world [...] *Socrates* took this idea from Anaxagoras, and it immediately became the predominant idea in philosophy, with the exception of *Epicurus*, who attributed all occurrences to chance" (*Die Vernunft in der Geschichte*, p. 38). Parmenides' "great affirmation", which identifies thinking with being, receives little attention from Hegel. Cf. *Geschichte der Philosophie* I (*Werke*, XIII, p. 296). Hegel discusses Aristotle's notion of "actuality" (*energeia*) in *Geschichte der Philosophie* II (*Werke* XIV, pp. 318–332).

118. Cf. *Logik* I, G.W. 11 pp. 17 ff.; *Enc.* A. 329; C. 413.
119. Cf. *Grl.* §132.
120. Cf. *Enc.* B, Preface: "Such a [scientific] development [of thought] proves itself to be nothing other than the recreation of that absolute content beyond which thinking (*Gedanke*) first strove and extended itself, but a recreation in the most peculiar, freest element of spirit".
121. Cf. *Grl.* §3+A and above pp. 6–10.
122. *Briefe* II, p. 242. All italics mine. Altenstein, to whom Hegel had written a similar letter to accompany the *Grundlinien* (*Briefe* II, pp. 237–238), understood Hegel's method well, as we see in his answer: "By emphasizing in this work (as you also do in your lectures) with the earnestness befitting science that one must grasp the present and actual and comprehend the rational in nature and history, it seems to me you provide philosophy with the only correct attitude toward reality, and thus you will most certainly succeed in protecting your listeners from the pernicious self-conceit which rejects existence without having known it and is satisfied, particularly with regard to the state, with arbitrarily constructing empty ideals".
123. With the expression "to the extent that" ("diese Abhandlung, insofern sie die Staatswissenschaft enthält", translated by Knox as "This book ..., containing as it does the science of the state"), Hegel indicates that this treatise contains more than just a philosophy of state in the strict sense; it also contains a philosophical grounding and explanation of the principles governing "abstract" right, the juridical aspects of morality, family life, the economy, the international order and political history. Cf. also the commentary given above on the title "Natural law *and the science of state* [or political science]" (*Naturrecht und Staatswissenschaft*).
124. This is one of the meanings of the second part of the *Philosophy of Right*, "Morality" (*Die Moralität*). Cf. also the passages quoted in the notes 108 and 114.
125. Cf. *Logik* I, G.W. 11, pp. 73–75 and (*e.g.*) *Enc.* C 171 *Zusatz*: "... when it is

said that an art work is beatiful or an action is good, the objects in question are compared with what they ought to be, i.e. with their concept".

126. Cf. *Dokumente zu Hegels Entwicklung*, p. 388 and the commentary in A.T.B. Peperzak, *Le jeune Hegel et la vision morale du monde*, The Hague 1969^2, p. 247.
127. *Aesopica* (ed. B.E. Perry, Urbana 1952), p. 334.
128. The second version can be found, for example, in an edition of Aesop by Halmius (Leipzig, Teubner 1854), n. 203b. Where Hegel found the Latin translation is unknown to me. Phaedrus did not include this fable. The quoted sentence was already in circulation in ancient times, as a proverb. Cf. the *Corpus Paroemiographorum Graecorum* II, pp. 101 (n. 86) and 461 (n. 100). In a review in which he defends this passage of the *Philosophy of Right* Hegel writes "Hic Rhodus, hic salta" instead of the translation containing "saltus". (*Berliner Schriften*, p. 402). Some information about this twofold translation is given by M. Haller, *System und Gesellschaft*, p. 198, Note 103.
129. The complete sentence reads: 'Ο *λόγος δηλοῖ ὅτι ὧν πρόχειρος ἡ δι' ἔργων πεῖρα, περί τούτων πᾶς λόγος περιττός ἐστιν.*
130. Ilting III, p. 821. Cf. also Ilting IV, p. 642 and *Philosophie der Weltgeschichte* (ed. Lasson), pp. 73–74.
131. Cf. also parts of *Grl.* §270A, *e.g.*, pp. 261–263 and §274 *Zusatz* (cf. Ilting III, pp. 753–756 and IV, p. 663).
132. An enlightening passage concerning Hegel's difficulties with subjectivism can also be found in Ilting IV, p. 83. After Hegel has clearly stated that " the existence and authority" of positive right say nothing about its value, and after having warned against the contrary misconception, that a constitution should be rejected simply because it claims authority and requires obedience or subjection (p. 82), he says:: "The laws must have the form to be indifferent to insight and caprice, yet it is up to the individuals to understand them. Laws [...] must withstand the test of reason. Thought, however, which gives laws wants to presuppose that every human being can judge what is right and good, that this is engraved in the human heart and that the standard for judging laws and constitutions is found in feeling. This is an unfortunate prejudice which especially in more recent times has caused much confusion and trouble [...]. If one recognizes [...] the demand [...] to comprehend the laws and compare them with the concept, this does not mean that to do so is easy or something immediately given. Rather one must recognize that positive laws can claim an impressive authority – that of many centuries, of the entire human race. The entire human race has worked at these laws, and it is not so easy to judge this work of the spirit, or to wish to be more clever than this world spirit. It is spirit alone which understands this; it should be our ambition to be equal to this and not to dismiss the matter with frivolous reflections."
133. The fact that Hegel translates *πήδημα* and *saltus/salta* by "dance" (*tanze*) is probably due to Goethe's influence, who included the fable in one of his *Zahme Xenien* (III, n. 2):

Willst du dich als Dichter beweisen,
So musst du nicht Helden noch Hirten preisen;
Hier ist Rhodus! Tanze, du Wicht,
Und der Gelegenheit schaff ein Gedicht!

134. In this paragraph, which in Knox's text is not distinct from the former, I have changed "mind" (for *Geist*) to "spirit" and "an actual world before our eyes" (*vorhandener Wirklichkeit*) to "existing actuality". Instead of "accidental" I prefer "contingent" as the translation of *das Zufällige* and the very literal "is in and for itself" (for *an und für sich ist*) to "exists absolutely".

135. *Berliner Schriften*, p. 402 (= *Werke* XVII, p. 227 = Glockner 20, p. 392). The symbol of the Rosicrucians was a golden cross with a rose in the middle.

136. R.K. Hočevar, *op.cit.*, p. 17. According to the *Encyclopedia Universalis* (XIV, pp. 439–441), a society of "Gold- and Rosicrucians of the older system" manifested itself in the German lands after 1777, with many (probably several thousand) members. Many freemasons were members of this society, or became members. J.R. Bischoffswerden and J.C. Wöllner, made Minister of War and Minister of State and Religion, respectively, by King Friedrich Wilhelm II of Prussia (1786–1797) after his ascent to the throne, were members before 1786 and initiated the king while he was still crown prince. The society died out in 1787. The *Enc. Universalis* cites various books from the Rosicrucian milieu for the years 1781–1788. "Rosicrucian" was also a much-used title in the 18th century for certain higher degrees of Freemasonry. Cf. also G. Lasson, "Kreuz und Rose: ein Interpretationsversuch", in: *Beiträge zur Hegel-Forschung* I, Berlin 1909, pp. 43–70. What Lasson writes there on p. 44 concerning the medallion which Hegel's students presented to him on his sixtieth birthday, which is also stated by M. Lenz, is not correct. The back of the medallion does not bear a rose and a cross, as they claim, but a radiant and winged genius between an old man, reading under an owl, and a woman carrying a staff ending in a cross to which the genius is pointing. The representation also symbolizes the unity of philosophy and theology. See the illustration in A. Gulyga, *Georg Wilhelm Friedrich Hegel*, Frankfurt a. M., 1974, 324 and cf. K. Schumm, *Bildnisse des Philosophen Georg Wilhelm Friedrich Hegel*, Stuttgart 1974, p. 39 and illustration 17. A correct description of the medallion is given in *Briefe* III, p. 462.

137. Cf. G. Lasson, *op.cit.*, p. 46 and K. Löwith, *Von Hegel zu Nietzsche*, pp. 28–43.

138. Cf. A. Chapelle, *Hegel et la religion* I, p. 21, where a letter from Luther concerning his coat of arms is quoted (and garbled due to several typographical errors).

139. *Des Christen Herz auf Rosen geht,*
Auch wenn's unterm Kreuze steht.
Lasson (*op.cit.* p. 46) incorrectly believes that Luther's coat of arms represents "the image of a rose in the middle of a cross". The relationship which Lasson sees between Luther's coat of arms and the writings of Johann Valentin Andrea, who is supposed to be the orginator of the various Rosicrucian societies, seems very dubious.

140. Ilting, p. 89. Hegel expressed his acceptance of the Lutheran interpretation of the christian faith on various occasions, e.g., in lectures on the philosophy of religion ("Wir Lutheraner – ich bin es und will es bleiben", *Werke* XIII, p. 89; Glockner 17, p. 105) and on the history of philosophy (*System und Geschichte der Philosophie*, p. 178). Cf. also *Berliner Schriften*, pp. 572–575. But cf. also Note 146.
141. *Philosophie der Religion* I, *Werke* XI, p. 277 (Glockner 15, p. 293). A slightly different version, which omits the reference to the rose and the cross, is found in the edition of Lasson: II, p. 37.
142. Lasson, *Beiträge* ... I, pp. 65–66. Cf. *Glauben und Wissen*, in: Gesammelte Werke II, pp. 413–414. Cf. also Hegel's commentary on the Lutheran song "God himself is dead" in *Philosophie der Religion* II (*Werke* XII, Glockner 16), pp. 306–307.
143. *Werke* XVII, p. 403 (Glockner 20, p. 448); cf. G. Lasson, "Kleine Notizen", in: *Beiträge zur Hegel-Forschung* II, p. 49.
144. Cf. strophes 8 and 9 of *die Geheimnisse.*
145. Knox's "speculative" (for *begreifendes*) has been changed to "conceptual"; "the world as it exists to-day" (for *die Gegenwart*) to "the present". The quotation-marks around Hegel's quote from the *Apocalyps* have been removed in accordance with the German text and the indeterminacy of the subject of the phrase *und darum ausgespien wird* (Knox: "it [reason] will will 'spue out of its mouth'") has been re-established by the translation "wil be spewed out" (by God? by Jesus? by the Spirit? by Reason? by reason?). "Average" seems to me a more adequate translation of *mittelmässig* than "only tolerable". "Actual" has been added to "world" in order to keep the connection with *Wirklichkeit.*
146. Cf. Note 97. Hegel's Protestantism, which he affirms in several places (cf. Note 140) and which he defends against the Pietistic theologians of his time, is placed in a peculiar light by the exhaustive transcription he gives of it in his religion, but also by private statements like the following: "You yourself know best how important scholarly institutions of learning are to Protestants; that they are as dear to them as churches and certainly just as valuable. Protestantism does not consist as much in a specific creed as in the spirit of reflection and of higher, more rational education, as opposed to a training geared to certain utilitarian ends (*Brauchbarkeiten*)" (letter to his friend Niethammer from November 3, 1810, *Briefe* I, p. 337) and: "Herein lies the difference between Catholicism and Protestantism. We have no laity; Protestantism is not entrusted to the hierarchical organization of a church but lies solely in universal insight and education... Our universities and schools are our churches. The pastors and religious services do not make up Protestantism like they do in the Catholic church" (to Niethammer July 12, 1816; *Briefe* II, p. 89).
147. *The Works of Francis Bacon*, London 1858, I, p. 430: "Quin potius certissimum est, atque experientia comprobatum, leves gustus in philosophia movere fortasse ad atheismum, sed pleniores haustus ad religionem reducere." According to a note by the editors this idea appears several times in Bacon's work.

148. "Divini ingenii vir Franciscus Baconus de Verulamio recte dixit philosophiam obiter libatam a Deo abducere, penitus haustam reducere ad eundem" (note by the editors to the passage quoted in Note 147.)
149. Cf. *Grl.* §§257–270.
150. How destructive this lack of understanding of the political is for religion as well is expressed by Hegel in *Enc.* C. 552A (at the end of the second paragraph): "True religion and true religiosity is based on ethicity only and is cogitative (i.e., increasingly conscious of the free universality of its concrete essence) ethicity. It is only proceeding from the ethical dimension that the idea of God as a free spirit is known; outside of the ethical spirit, therefore, it is useless to search for true religion and religiosity." With the phrases "as something neither cold nor hot" and "will be spewed" out Hegel makes an allusion to the *Book of Revelation* 3, 15–16, where "Amen" reproaches the church of Laodicea: "I know thy works, that thou art neither cold nor hot: I would thou wert cold or hot. So then, because thou art lukewarm, and neither cold nor hot, I will spue thee out of my mouth."
151. In the conversation with the disciple following on the conversation with Faust, from which a few verses have been quoted in Note 66, Mephistopheles says:

    Grau, teuer Freund, ist alle Theorie,
    Und grün des Lebens goldner Baum.

152. Cf. the beginning of the oration (quoted several times above) with which Hegel started his lectures in Heidelberg on October 28, 1818 (*System und Geschichte der Philosophie*, pp. 3–4): As long as the *Weltgeist* was so busy with the reality of the little needs of everyday life and the major interests and battles of politics it could "not turn inward and gather itself into itself." But now (after 1815) it is once again possible that we "keep" ourselves "free for the higher inner life, the purer spirituality." "*Now, since* this current of actuality is broken, since the German nation *has torn itself free from* the most coarse, since it *has saved its nationality, the ground of all vital life*, so we may hope that besides the *state*, which takes up all interest into itself, the *church*, too, can elevate itself; that besides the *secular realm*, to which thought and effort have been dedicated until now, the *realm of God* will again be considered, in other words that besides the *political and other* interests tied to the common *reality, pure science, the free rational world of the spirit, will also flourish again*." In his Berlin oration of October 22, 1818 (*Berliner Schriften*, pp. 3–4), Hegel repeated a great part of this passage, but – and this in connection with the quotations in Note 146 is revealing – substituting "the *free realm of thought*" for "the church" and "the realm of God", while referring to the state as the "regiment of the *actual* (*wirklichen*) world." Apparently Hegel no longer wanted to indicate so clearly his identification of the "realm of God" with the domain of philosophy. The idea that philosophy is reflection after the fact is also retained in a copy of the course on the history of philosophy by Griesheim, now the property of the Staatsbibliothek Preussischer Kulturbesitz in Berlin (Ms. germ. qu. 540). On p. 40 of the manuscript it is stated that a philosophy ("as an ideal world to which

thought escapes") begins when the "real world" of ethicity enters a period of "decay" (*Verderben*). "Philosophy begins with the decline of a real world; when philosophy appears with its abstractions, *painting grey in grey* [my emphasis], the freshness of youth vibrance is already gone and its reconciliation is not a reconciliation in reality but in the ideal world." These passages must also be related to the rise and fall of peoples which Hegel discusses in *Grl.* §§343 and 347 and, more extensively, in *Die Vernunft in der Geschichte*, pp. 67–69. Philosophy is the work of old age, a sign that the nation in which it blooms is perishing.

153. Cf. Hegel's very extensive discussion of Plato's *Republic* in *Geschichte der Philosophie* II, *Werke* XIV (Glockner 18), pp. 269–296 and in: *Leçons sur Platon; texte inédit 1825–1826* (ed. J.C. Vieillard-Baron), Paris 1976, pp. 122–134.

154. As I hope to show in a commentary on the whole of the *Philosophy of Right*, the end of this book makes clear the degree to which Hegel's anti-prophetism leads to unsolved problems and the necessity of an abstract *Ought* on a world-wide level.

155. I changed "personal" (for *subjektiv*) into "subjective" and "capricious" (*beliebig*) into "arbitrary".

156. *Enc.*, p. 4. Although it does not lead to "true understanding" and is "unpopular and even unpleasant", Hegel still considers this unscientific speaking and writing necessary and useful as an aid to gaining access to scientific speaking and writing. But how can the relation between these two kinds of language be understood? This is thematized by Hegel in *Enc.* A. 368–387; BC. 445–468.

157. *Berliner Schriften*, p. 355.

BIBLIOGRAPHY

I. Texts by Hegel

Hegel's earliest works (*Jugendschriften*) are quoted from H. Nohl's edition of *Hegel's theologische Jugendschriften*, Tübingen 1907, and J. Hoffmeister's edition of *Dokumente zu Hegels Entwicklung*, Stuttgart 1936, 1974².

What Hegel wrote in Jena (1801–1807) until the *Phenomenology of Spirit* (*Phänomenologie des Geistes*) is quoted from the *Gesammelte Werke*, Hamburg 1968 ff. For all the works published by Lasson and Hoffmeister in their "critical edition" of the collected works I follow their text (except for the *Encyklopädie*, see below). The *Logic* is also quoted from the *Gesammelte Werke* (vols. 11 and 12).

For the *Philosophy of Right* I use the text of the fourth edition, Hamburg 1967. Hegel's marginal notes and his lectures on the philosophy of right of 1818–19, 1822–23, 1824–25 and 1831 have been published by K.H. Ilting in G.W.F. Hegel, *Vorlesungen über Rechtsphilosophie 1818–1831*, 4 volumes, Stuttgart 1973–1974. – D. Henrich has published student notes of Hegel's lecture of 1819–20 in G.W.F. Hegel, *Philosophie des Rechts. Die Vorlesung von 1819/20 in einer Nachschrift*, Frankfurt 1983. The notes of Wannenman taken during Hegel's lecture of 1817–18 in Heidelberg have been published by the staff of the Hegel-Archiv (C. Becker e.a.) as G.W.F. Hegel, *Vorlesungen über Naturrecht und Staatswissenschaft*. Heidelberg 1817/18 mit Nachträgen aus der Vorlesung 1818/19. Nachgeschrieben von Wannenman, Hamburg 1983, and by K.H. Ilting, who combined it with a new edition of Homeyer's notes of 1818/19 in: G.W.F. Hegel, *Die Philosophie des Rechts*. Die Mitschriften Wannenman (Heidelberg 1817/18 und Homeyer (Berlin 1818/19, Stuttgart 1983.

The text of the third edition of Hegel's *Enzyklopädie der philosophischen Wissenschaften* (Berlin 1830), prepared by Hegel himself, is quoted from F. Nicolins and O. Pöggelers edition in the *Philosophische Bibliothek*, Hamburg 1959. Hegel's other works are quoted and translated from the *Jubiläumsausgabe* by H. Glockner (*Sämtliche Werke* I–XX, Stuttgart 1927–1930), which is to a great extent a re-issue of the *Werke* in the 19 volumes of the "*Vollständige Ausgabe*" by an "association of friends of the deceased", Berlin 1832–1887. Hegel's letters are quoted from J. Hoffmeister (ed.), *Briefe von und an Hegel*, 4 volumes, Hamburg 1961[2].

II. A selection from the literature

E. Angehrn, *Freiheit und System bei Hegel*, Berlin 1977.

S. Avineri, *Hegel's Theory of the Modern State*, Cambridge 1972.

N. Bobbio, "Hegel e il diritto", in: F. Tessitore (ed.), *Incidenza di Hegel*, Salerno 1970, p. 215–250.

R. Bodei, "Filosofia e politica nello Hegel berlinese", in: F. Tessitore (ed.), *Incidenza di Hegel*, Salerno 1970, p. 309–339.

B. Bourgeois, *La pensée politique de Hegel*, Paris 1969.

P. Brückner, "*....bewahre uns Gott in Deutschland vor irgendeiner Revolution!*", Berlin 1975.

C. Cesa, *Hegel Filosofo Politico*, Napoli 1976.

C. Cesa, "Doveri universali e doveri di Stato. Considerazioni sull'etica di Hegel", in: *Rivista di Filosofia* 68 (1977), p. 30–48.

C. Cesa, Introduzione, in: C. Cesa (ed.), *Il pensiero politico di Hegel. Guida storica e critica*, Roma 1979, p. V–XLIV.

K. Düsing, "Politische Ethik bei Plato und Hegel", in: *Hegel-Studien* 19 (1984), p. 95–145.

E. Fleischmann, *La philosophie politique de Hegel*, Paris 1964.

H.F. Fulda, "Zum Theorietypus der Hegelschen Rechtsphilosophie", in: D. Henrich & R.P. Horstmann (eds.), *Hegels Philosophie des Rechts; Die Theorie der Rechtsformen und ihre Logik*, Stuttgart 1982, pp. 393–427.

M. Haller, *System und Gesellschaft*, Stuttgart 1981 (p. 188–213 are dedicated to the Preface of Hegel's Grundlinien).

D. Henrich, "Logische Form und reale Totalität", in: D. Henrich & R.P. Horstmann, (eds.), *Hegels Philosophie des Rechts; Die Theorie der Rechtsformen und ihre Logik*, Stuttgart 1982, p. 428–450.

D. Henrich, "Einleitung des Herausgebers: "Vernunft in Verwirklichung" and "Nachtrag", in: G.W.F. Hegel, *Philosophie des Rechts. Die Vorlesung von 1819/20 in einer Nachschrift*, Frankfurt 1983, p. 9–39 and 371–376.

R.K. Hočevar, *Hegel und der Preussische Staat*, München 1973.

K.H. Ilting, *Einleitung. Die "Rechtsphilosophie" von 1820 und Hegels Vorlesungen über Rechtsphilosophie*, in: G.W.F. Hegel, *Vorlesungen über Rechtsphilosophie 1818–1831*, Stuttgart 1973 ff., vol. I, p. 23–126.

K.H. Ilting, "Rechtsphilosophie als Phänomenologie des Bewusstseins

der Freiheit", in: D. Henrich & R.P. Horstmann (eds.), *Hegels Philosophie des Rechts; Die Theorie der Rechtsformen und ihre Logik*, Stuttgart 1982, p. 225–254.
K.H. Ilting, *Einleitung des Herausgebers. Die neue Quellenlage*, in: G.W.F. Hegel, *Die Philosophie des Rechts. Die Mitschriften Wannenmann (Heidelberg 1817/18) und Homeyer (Berlin 1818/1819)*, Stuttgart 1983, p. 17–34.
R. Koselleck, "Staat und Gesellschaft in Preussen 1815–1848", in: Wehler (ed.), *Moderne Sozialgeschichte*, Berlin 1966, p. 55–84.
R. Koselleck, *Preussen zwischen Reform und Revolution*, Stuttgart 1965[1]; 1975[2].
M. Lenz, *Geschichte der königlichen Friedrich-Wilhelms-Universität zu Berlin*, 4 vols., Halle 1910.
D. Losurdo, *Hegel. Questione Nazionale. Restaurazione. Presupposti e sviluppi di una battaglia politica*, Urbino 1983.
G. Lübbe-Wolff, "Hegels Staatsrecht als Stellungnahme im ersten Preussischen Verfassungskampf", in: *Zeitschrift für philosophische Forschung* 35 (1981), p. 476–501.
H.C. Lucas & U. Rameil, "Furcht vor der Zenzur. Zur Entstehungs- und Druckgeschichte von Hegels Grundlinien der Philosophie des Rechts", in: *Hegel-Studien* 15 (1980), p. 63–93.
G. Marini, "La polemica con la scuola storica nella Filosofia de diritto hegeliana", in: *Rivista di Filosofia* 68 (1977), p. 169–204.
G. Marini, *Libertà soggettiva e libertá oggettiva nella "Filosofia del diritto" hegeliana*, Napoli 1978.
H. Ottman, *Individuum und Gesellschaft bei Hegel*, vol. I: *Hegel im Spiegel der Interpretationen*, Berlin 1977.
H. Ottman, "Hegels Rechtsphilosophie und das Problem der Akkomodation", in: *Zeitschrift für philosophische Forschung* 33 (1979), p. 227–243.
H. Ottman, "Hegel und die Politik. Zur Kritik der politischen Hegellegenden", in: *Zeitschrift für Politik* 26 (1979), p. 235–253.
Z.A. Pelczynski, "An Introductory Essay", in: T.M. Knox & Pelczynski (eds.), *Hegel's Political Writings*, Oxford 1964, p. 5–137.
A.Th. Peperzak, *Le jeune Hegel et la vision morale du monde*, The Hague 1969[2].
A.Th. Peperzak, "Der Staat und Ich", in: *Hegel-Jahrbuch* 1975, Köln 1976, p. 83–104.
A.Th. Peperzak, "Religion et politique dans la philosophie de Hegel", in: G. Planty-Bonjour (ed.), *Hegel et la Religion*, Paris 1982, p. 37–76.
A.Th. Peperzak, "Zur Hegelschen Ethik", in: D. Henrich & R.P. Horstmann (eds.), *Hegels Philosophie des Rechts; Die Theorie der Rechtsformen und ihre Logik*, Stuttgart 1982, p. 103–131.
A.Th. Peperzak, "Hegels Pflichten- und Tugendlehre", in: *Hegel-Studien* 17 (1982), p. 97–117.

A.Th. Peperzak, "The Foundations of Ethics according to Hegel", in: *International Philosophical Quarterly* 23 (1983), p. 349–365.
O. Pöggeler, "Einleitung" in: G.W.F. Hegel, *Vorlesungen über Naturrecht und Staatswissenschaft. Heidelberg 1817/18 mit Nachträgen aus der Vorlesung 1818/19. Nachgeschrieben von P. Wannenmann*, Hamburg 1983, p. IX–XLVIII.
M. Riedel (eds.), *Materialien zu Hegels Rechtsphilosophie*, Frankfurt 1975.
M. Riedel, *Zwischen Tradition und Revolution. Studien zu Hegels Rechtsphilosophie*, Stuttgart 1982 (enlarged edition of *Studien zu Hegels Rechtsphilosophie*, Frankfurt 1969).
D. Rosenfield, *Politique et Liberté. Une étude sur la structure logique de la Philosophie du Droit de Hegel*, Paris 1984.
K. Rosenkranz, *Hegel als Deutscher Nationalphilosoph*, Leipzig 1870.
F. Rosenzweig, *Hegel und der Staat*, 2 vols., München 1920.
L. Siep, "Intersubjektivität, Recht und Staat in Hegels 'Grundlinien der Philosophie des Rechts'", in: D. Henrich & R.P. Horstmann (eds.), *Hegels Philosophie des Rechts; Die Theorie der Rechtsformen und ihre Logik*, Stuttgart 1982, p. 255–276.
W. Simon, *The Failure of the Prussian Reform Movement 1807–1819*, Ithaca 1955.
E. Weil, *Hegel et l'Etat*, Paris 1950.
E. Weil, *Hegel et la philosophie du Droit*, Paris 1979.

Why People Pay Taxes